"If Jim Henson, Martha Stewart, and Weird Al were to morph into one being, it would be Rachel Faucett. The creativity, enthusiasm, style, and irreverence she brings to *Handmade Charlotte* is inspired, and this book is what the world needs now."

—HALLE STANFORD, PRESIDENT OF TELEVISION AT THE JIM HENSON COMPANY

"Rachel is the queen of crafting with kids! I have looked to her for years on ideas and inspiration on how to keep my kids entertained in fun and creative ways. This book is truly a must-have to any family's home library."

—JOY CHO, FOUNDER AND CREATIVE DIRECTOR OF OH JOY!

"*Handmade Charlotte* has become *the* go-to for top-quality crafting and activities for kids, and their playbook is no exception. Just like the blog we've all come to know and love, this book leaves me thinking 'How did they come up with that?!' over and over again. I cannot wait for it to become the crafting companion for my son!"

—BRITTANY JEPSEN, FOUNDER AND CREATIVE DIRECTOR OF THE HOUSE THAT LARS BUILT

"Ever wondered how to foster creativity in your kids? This is it! Rachel Faucett's collection of projects brings grins and gasps of delight with every page turn. These crafts are true imagination builders, and the perfect way for kids to exercise creative muscles—you can practically see the gears turning in their head as they choose something to work on and figure out what materials they can use or reuse. Rachel is an artistic genius who understands children, and how they relate to art, at a core level. I was hoping for a *Handmade Charlotte* craft book for ages, and this was beyond my very high expectations."

—GABRIELLE BLAIR, BESTSELLING AUTHOR, FOUNDER OF DESIGNMOM.COM AND ALT SUMMIT, AND MOTHER OF SIX

"Every time I'm around Rachel, her excitement for life makes me want to go out and chase all my wildest dreams. It's no surprise that her book holds the key to not only encouraging childhood curiosity but sparking creativity in the whole family, so you can make memories together, today."

—KELLY MINDELL, FOUNDER AND CREATIVE DIRECTOR OF STUDIO DIY

"Rachel Faucett is a creative magician who can conjure rainbows and happiness from pasta and pipe cleaners. I'd thought I'd seen it all, but I truly gasped with delight every time I turned the page in her *amazing* book. Kids and grown-ups will have so much fun creating everything in this encyclopedia of crafty fun!"

—JODI LEVINE, FOUNDER AND CREATIVE DIRECTOR OF SUPER MAKE IT

"*The Handmade Charlotte Playbook* is pure, packaged sunshine. For all of us who struggle to color between the lines, Rachel will have you rediscovering creative instincts you didn't know existed."

—JANE MOSBACHER MORRIS, FOUNDER AND CEO OF TO THE MARKET AND AUTHOR OF
BUY THE CHANGE YOU WANT TO SEE (PENGUIN RANDOM HOUSE, JANUARY 2019)

"The boundless creativity of Rachel Faucett and *Handmade Charlotte* is mind-blowing! Her crafts turn the most mundane and overlooked household items into artful treasures. With crafts full of humor, joy, and beauty, kids will be delighted flipping from one page to the next!"

—AMANDA KINGLOFF, FORMER LIFESTYLE DIRECTOR
AT *PARENTS* MAGAZINE AND FOUNDER OF PROJECT KID

the
HANDMADE
CHARLOTTE
PLAYBOOK

tarcherperigee

an imprint of Penguin Random House LLC
penguinrandomhouse.com

Most TarcherPerigee books are available at special quantity discounts for bulk purchase for sales promotions, premiums, fund-raising, and educational needs. Special books or book excerpts also can be created to fit specific needs. For details, write: SpecialMarkets@penguinrandomhouse.com.

Library of Congress Cataloging-in-Publication Data

Names: Faucett, Rachel, author.
Title: The Handmade Charlotte playbook: crafts, games, and recipes for
families to do together throughout the year / Rachel Faucett.
Description: New York: TarcherPerigee an imprint of Penguin Random House
LLC, 2020.
Identifiers: LCCN 2020015650 (print) | LCCN 2020015651 (ebook) |
ISBN 9780143133636 (paperback) | ISBN 9780525505426 (ebook)
Subjects: LCSH: Family recreation. | Handicraft. | Cooking.
Classification: LCC GV182.8 .F39 2020 (print) | LCC GV182.8 (ebook) |
DDC 790.1/91—dc23
LC record available at https://lccn.loc.gov/2020015650
LC ebook record available at https://lccn.loc.gov/2020015651

Printed in China
10 9 8 7 6 5 4 3 2 1

Book design by Lorie Pagnozzi

Composition by Neuwirth & Associates, Inc.

To our children

IZZY, JONAH, MURPHY, CHARLOTTE, AND NOAH
for sharing their uninhibited, beautiful minds
with us every day and letting us experience the
kind of love that transcends words.

To our parents

NEILL, BILLA, AND PATRICIA
You believed, so we believed.

And now these three remain: faith, hope, and love.
But the greatest of these is love.

1 CORINTHIANS 13:13

CONTENTS

INTRODUCTION   1   HOW TO USE THIS BOOK   2

A

ABACUS CANDY   5

ACORN MATCHING GAME   7

ALLIGATOR PUPPET   10

ALPHABET MAGNETS   15

AWARD RIBBONS   17

B

BALLOON POP GAME   21

BANANA PUPPETS   23

BEETLES   26

BINOCULARS   31

BIRD FEEDER   33

BUMBLEBEE SLIME BOXES   36

BUNNY CUPCAKES   40

BETTER BLONDIES   43

C

CACTUS   47

CALLA LILIES   50

COOKIE-CUTTER CANDY POPS   53

CHARCOAL   59

CHEWY CHECKERS   60

CHURRO ACTION FIGURES   63

CUCUMBER CAKES   66

D

DAFFODIL CUPCAKES   71

DIORAMAS   72

DIVER PUPPET   75

DONUT BUNNIES   79

E

EGG PARTY FAVORS 83

EASY EMBROIDERY 85

ENVELOPES 89

ERASER PIÑATA 91

F

FINGERPRINT PUMPKINS 97

FLOWER PAPER CLIPS 99

FORTUNE COOKIES 103

FRIENDSHIP BRACELETS 106

FLAMINGOS 111

FANCY FRENCH TOAST 115

G

GRADUATION OWLS 118

GUMDROP SWANS 123

GRANOLA BARS 127

H

HAIR CHARMS 131

HALF MILK 133

HAPPY MAIL PENCIL CASE 135

HEY HEY CROSS-STITCH MAGNETS 115

HORSE IN THE FOREST CAKE 143

HOT POTATO 145

I

ICE-CREAM CHARMS 151

ICE-CREAM PUPPET 154

ICE-POP MONSTERS 157

INVISIBLE INK 159

ICE CREAM 161

J

JAZZY CASSETTE PEOPLE 165

JOLLY STORAGE JARS 167

JAM 170

K

KEY CHAINS 175

KISS ART 178

KITTEN CLUTCHES 180

KOKESHI DOLL STIR STICKS 185

L

LANTERNS 189

LEAF PAINTING 191

LEANING TOWERS OF TRAPEZE 193

LOVELY LLAMAS 195

LOBSTER CUPCAKES 199

LEMON BARS 201

M

MANDALA COOKIE TINS 205

MONOGRAMS 207

MOON IN YOUR ROOM 211

MOUSE GIFT BOX 215

MILK SHAKE 217

MONKEY BREAD 219

N

NATURE BINGO 223

NIGHT SKY FLASHLIGHT 224

NOODLE PARTY 227

NEAPOLITAN TREATS 231

O

OLIVE STRESS BALLS 235

OLIVE TRADING BEADS 237

ORNAMENTS 239

OLIVE OIL CHERRY CAKE 243

P

PAPER BAG PUPPETS 247

PASTA PLANTS 251

PATCHES 252

PEANUT PARTY FAVORS 255

PING-PONG BUNNY CUPCAKE TOPPERS 259

PLAY CLAY SWEET SHOP 263

PRETZEL NECKLACE 265

Q

QUEEN OF HEARTS PUPPET 271

QUILT MAGNETS 275

R

RAINBOW MACARONI 281

RAINBOW PUPPET 283

ROCK PUZZLE 287

ROCKS ON THE BEACH 289

RASPBERRY-MANGO SMOOTHIES 291

S

SALAD SPINNER PLATES 295

SAND MILL 297

SEWING CARDS 301

SHIBORI WALL HANGINGS 305

SKEE-BALL 307

SOLAR SYSTEM NECKLACE 311

STRIPY STORAGE 315

SWISS CHEESE FORT 319

SLAB PIE 321

T

TANGRAM PIÑATA   327

TIE-DYE TAPESTRIES   331

TOPS   335

TREE ORNAMENTS   337

TURKEY PARTY FAVORS   339

U

UNDER THE SEA
MACARONI WREATH   345

UNEXPECTED ENCOURAGEMENT   348

UNICORN PUPPET   351

URCHIN ICE CREAM   355

UPSIDE-DOWN PINEAPPLE CAKE   357

V

VALENTINE'S DAY WREATH   361

VEGGIE BLOCKS   363

VEGGIE KNOTS   365

VICTORY LAP VILLAGE   369

W

WALNUT LLAMA ORNAMENTS   373

WALRUS COSTUME   374

WATERCOLOR WINDSOCKS   377

WATERMELON CHARMS   381

WISH UPON A WREATH CAKE   385

X

XYLOPHONE   389

XOXO SUGAR COOKIES   393

Y

YUMMY YOGURT PARFAITS   397

Z

ZUCCHINI BREAD   401

ZUCCHINI CUPCAKES   402

ACKNOWLEDGMENTS   405   PHOTO CREDITS   407   PROJECT INDEX BY TYPE   411

RECIPE INDEX BY TYPE   413   SEASONAL AND HOLIDAY INDEX   415   ABOUT THE AUTHOR   419

INTRODUCTION

I can still remember, as if it were yesterday, the lazy afternoons I spent as a child thumbing through the well-worn pages of the Childcraft anthology's ninth volume, *Make and Do*. Carved soap turtles, refrigerator box submarines . . . The book provided the key to a brave new world where ordinary things could be turned into something extraordinary. I would come home from school and immediately hunt for the book, often finding it on the floor in the corner of my room, next to the flashlight I'd used to read it the night before, or under the kitchen table. The only place you could guarantee I wouldn't find it was on a bookshelf. But isn't that true of all great books? *Make and Do* wasn't just a book; it was a constant companion.

The Handmade Charlotte Playbook is intended to be just such a companion. The supplies you'll need are inexpensive, readily available, and easy to find. The step-by-step instructions are easy to follow, but you can also modify them to fit the particular supplies you have on hand or your own creative vision. The objective is for you to achieve a sense of happiness when you're making our crafts with your family. The privilege of getting this behind-the-scenes look at our children's ingenuity is pure gold. Not only do we gain insight and perspective from their boundless creativity, we learn who they are, what's on their minds, and what issues they might be grappling with. We play together, learn together, grow together. And together, we experience a rewarding sense of accomplishment—in this case, from working on activities where the emphasis is on fun, and perfection is not the goal.

Keep this playbook on your kitchen table, not tucked away on a bookshelf. A quick flip through its pages can inspire a new creative journey. Use it as a starting point to intuitively construct your own serendipitous experiences. And remember, perfection is not the point. It's about childlike exploration, not a preconceived notion of excellence.

Now let's start exploring!

HOW TO USE
THIS BOOK

A Start with the letter A and make your way to Z, creating lifelong memories along the way;

B Turn to the back of the book for an index of projects listed by category (page 411), recipes listed by type (page 413), or projects and recipes categorized by seasons and holidays (page 415); or

C Close your eyes, open the book, and let the pages fall where they may!

CHAPTER 1

ABACUS CANDY

Math homework is much sweeter when you have a candy calculator. Believe it or not, this abacus really works! Just be sure to subtract the candies you eat along the way.

SUPPLIES

10 wooden skewers

Four 12-inch-long wooden dowels

String

Ruler

Hot-glue gun and glue

Scissors

Craft knife

100 Life Savers or other ring-shaped hard candies

DIRECTIONS

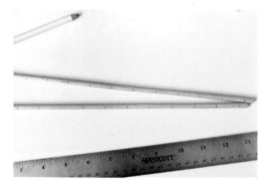 

1. Measure in ½ inch from each end of a dowel, and mark a tick on the dowel. Make ticks at 1-inch intervals between your first two marks, so the dowel has 12 ticks. Repeat with a second dowel.

2. Cut the remaining 2 dowels down to about 10 inches, or no longer than the length of your wooden skewers. Hot glue the 2 short dowels to the end tick marks on the first two dowels, making a rectangle. Secure the glued joints with string.

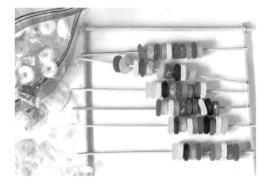 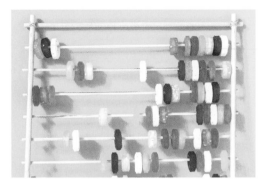

3. Cut the wooden skewers down to about 10 inches long, so they fit across the dowel frame. Unwrap the candies, and place 10 candies onto each of the wooden skewers.

4. Hot glue the wooden skewers onto the dowels, placing each end of the skewers on the tick marks you made in the first step. Be sure to use enough glue to secure the skewers well—the candies are heavier than you think! (For additional strength, tie strings around these joints as well, if you like.) Once the glue has cooled and set, count away!

TIPS

* The unwrapped candies won't last forever, but if treated with care, they should last for a few homework sessions before they're gobbled up!

* Be careful not to get hot glue on the candies themselves. Hot glue is not edible!

* Coat the candies with a sealant if you don't plan to eat them and just want a playful-looking abacus.

ACORN MATCHING GAME

Memory match has never been more fun! Gather a collection of empty acorn tops on your next walk, and give them a sparkling makeover with paint and glitter.

About 20 empty acorn tops

Multisurface acrylic
paint in 5 colors

Mod Podge

Glitter to match
the paint colors

Paintbrushes

DIRECTIONS

1. Paint the insides of the acorn tops. Be sure to paint only 2 acorns in each color, so that you have about 10 matching pairs. Let dry.

2. Apply a coat of Mod Podge to the painted acorn interiors.

TIPS FOR GAME PLAY

* Arrange the acorn tops colored-sides down on a wooden tray. Make sure to mix them up so you don't remember where the matches are! Play with a friend, taking turns trying to pick matching acorn tops.

* Store the finished acorns in a small bag, box, or tray. A shallow tray or box lid makes an excellent base to play the matching game in and allows for quick tidy-up.

* If you don't have many oak trees where you live, make a memory match game using rocks instead. In this case, paint only one side of each rock, so the color isn't visible from the top.

3. While the Mod Podge is still wet, sprinkle the acorn tops with glitter that matches the paint underneath. Let dry.

ALLIGATOR PUPPET

Almost anything can be made into a puppet, including repurposed household recyclables. This friendly alligator gives an empty egg carton a whole new life—the bumpy bottom looks just like teeth!

SUPPLIES

Cardboard egg carton

Acrylic paint
(green, white, and pink)

Pink felt

Paintbrushes

Scissors

Hot-glue gun and glue

Green craft foam

2 Ping-Pong balls

Black permanent marker

DIRECTIONS

1. Cut along the hinge of the cardboard egg carton to separate the top and bottom. Paint the top green on the outside and pink on the inside; let the paint dry. Paint the outside of the bumpy bottom half white, and let the paint dry.

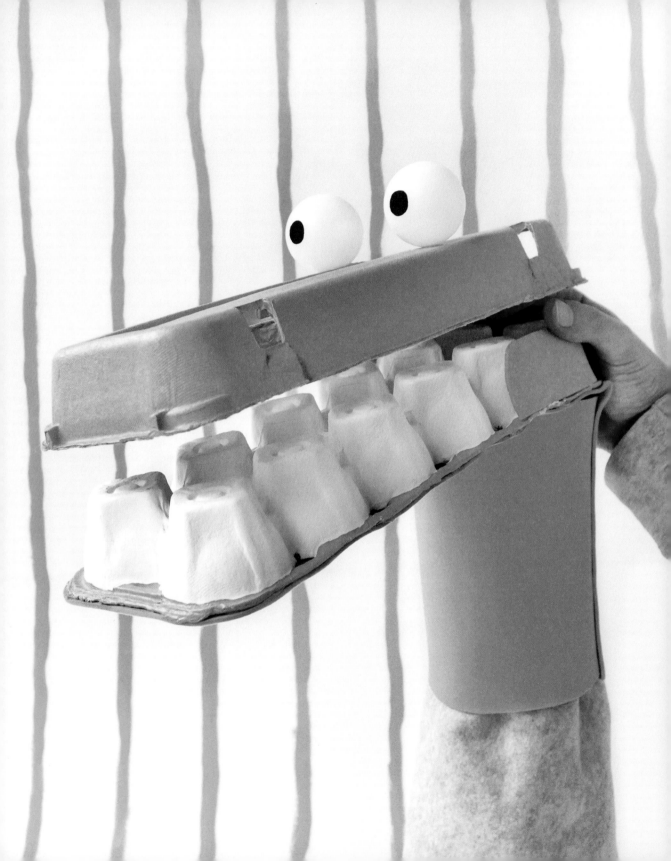

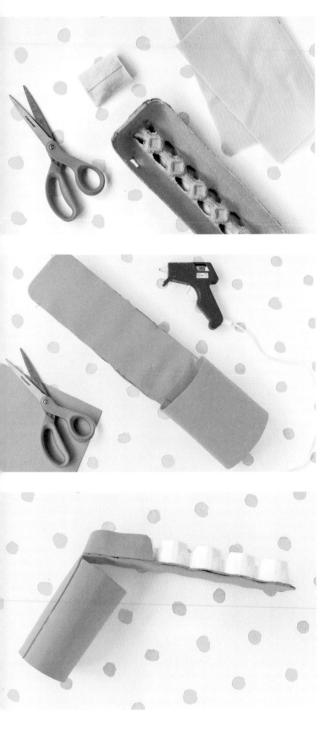

2. Cut a 3 by 7-inch rectangle of pink felt, and roll it into a tube that fits snugly around your 3 middle fingers. Hot glue the edges of the felt into a pink felt pocket, and then hot glue it to the center of one end of the pink side of the egg carton top.

3. Trace the bumpy white bottom of the egg carton onto green craft foam, extending it about 8 inches longer on one end, and cut out the foam. Hot glue the green foam to the bottom of the egg carton so that the excess foam hangs off the end as a tab. Cut an 8 by 12-inch rectangle of green foam, and hot glue one of the 8-inch sides onto the 8-inch tab.

4. Take the other end of the rectangle, and form a tube that fits your forearm snugly. Hot glue the other end of the rectangle to the tab to secure the tube.

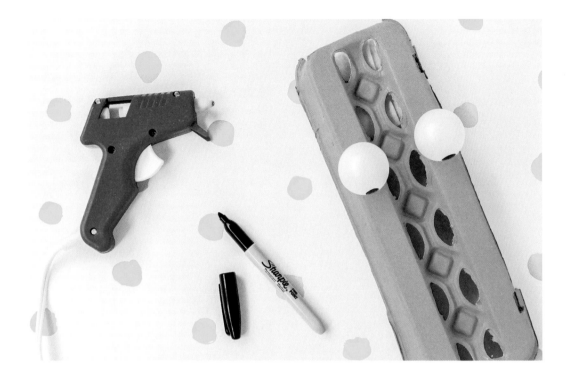

5. Hot glue the Ping-Pong balls onto the green side of the egg carton top, at the same end as the pink felt pocket. Draw pupils onto the Ping-Pong balls with black permanent marker.

HOW TO USE PUPPET

* Put the three middle fingers of your dominant hand into the felt pink pocket to control the top jaw of the alligator.

* Make a fist with your other hand, and fit it into the green tube on the bottom jaw.

* Rest the two pieces together to complete the alligator's face, and use the thumb and pinky finger of your dominant hand to grip the bottom jaw.

* While gripping, lift your three middle fingers so the alligator's jaw will open and close.

ALPHABET MAGNETS

Kids learning their ABCs will love these rainbow-hued magnets. Put a colorful spin on a classic craft using clay, cookie cutters, magnets, and glue. Put them on your fridge or on a cookie sheet, and let the emerging readers in your family use them to turn letters into words.

SUPPLIES

Polymer clay	Letter-shaped cookie cutters	Glue
Rolling pin	Baking sheet	Magnets

DIRECTIONS

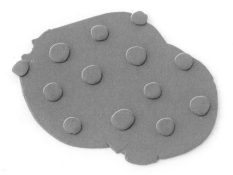

1. Check the directions on the polymer clay packaging, and preheat the oven to the temperature specified. Knead the polymer clay until it is soft and malleable. Use the rolling pin to flatten the clay so that it's ¼ to ½ inch thick. Place little balls of contrasting-colored clay on top, and then roll them flat to form polka dots.

2. Using the letter-shaped cookie cutters, cut out each letter of the alphabet from the clay.

3. Place the letters on the baking sheet, and bake according to the directions on the polymer clay packaging.

4. Let the letters cool.

5. Glue magnets to the back of each letter.

AWARD RIBBONS

Have you ever seen photos of vintage horse show ribbons? The colors, shapes, and details are unbelievable! Make your own ribbons out of candy and cookies, and you've got some tasty, award-winning rainbow treats to bring to a county fair or pony party.

Sour belt candy or
Bubble Tape gum

Scissors

Mini vanilla wafer cookies

DIRECTIONS

1. Use kitchen scissors to cut the sour belt candy or Bubble Tape gum into 2¼-inch-long strips. Cut a small triangle out of the bottom of each strip (cut in at an angle from each corner so the cuts meet in the middle).

2. Arrange 1, 2, or 3 sour strips under a mini vanilla wafer cookie to look like a prize ribbon. Play with the colors and arrangement.

3. Place the edible "prize ribbon" on a cake, cupcake, brownie, pie, etc.

CHAPTER 2

BALLOON POP GAME

Practice your aim with this giant handmade balloon pop game. Only a few supplies are needed to make a big statement with this simple craft.

SUPPLIES

Pencil

White foam core

Craft knife

50 balloons
(red, white, and blue)

Paper clips

Hot-glue gun and glue

Wooden dowels

Scissors

Colored Cardstock

DIRECTIONS

1. Draw a giant circle on the foam core, and cut it out with a craft knife. In the circle's center, make a small "X" through the foam core.

2. Blow up a balloon, and feed the knotted end through the "X" in the foam core. Repeat this process, working in circles to cover the entire foam core target with balloons. Take a step back, and check the balloon placement. Cut additional holes if you need to rearrange the balloons.

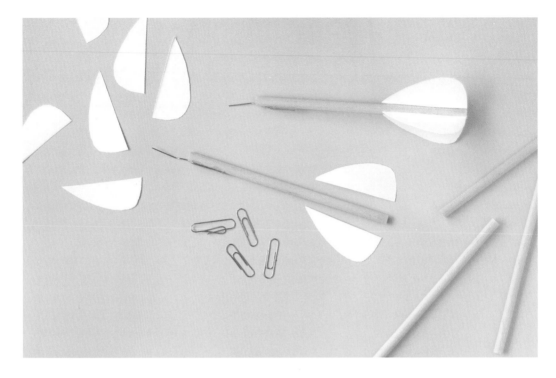

3. To make the darts, unfold one end of a paper clip, and hot glue the folded end to the end of a short wooden dowel. Cut paper fins from cardstock, and hot glue them onto the other end of the dowel, placing them on opposite sides of the dowel. Repeat to make several darts.

GAMEPLAY TIPS

* To play, take turns throwing arrows at the bull's-eye, and keep track of who pops the most balloons!

* The dart's tip needs to be pointy enough to pop a balloon, but keep in mind the age of your players (safety first!) and if you're playing indoors or outdoors (you don't want to damage any furniture or scratch paint off the wall).

* The balloons will shrink overnight—keep playing until you pop them all!

BANANA PUPPETS

Paint a fruit bowl full of banana puppets, and parade them around the house! Aluminum foil makes an excellent sculpting medium for beginners since it's affordable and only needs a gentle touch.

Aluminum foil		Paintbrushes		Googly eyes
Acrylic paint (yellow and brown)		White glue		Ice-pop sticks
		Clear tape		

DIRECTIONS

1. Cut a piece of aluminum foil into an approximately 18 by 12-inch rectangle. Roll the foil loosely into a tube.

2. Shape the foil gently, pinching each end, giving it a slight curve and keeping the foil edge to the back. Tape an ice-pop stick onto the back of the foil banana.

3. Paint the bananas yellow. Paint the ends brown to look like stems. Let dry completely.

4. Glue googly eyes onto each banana.

BEETLES

Deck the walls with a gallery of glittery bugs. Start with a printed picture for a quick project, or design your own new species. Make an entire collection of shadowboxes, and you'll have a great start to your own personal science museum.

SUPPLIES

Mod Podge	Glitter (various colors)	Box lid
Large printouts of beetles and bugs	Paintbrushes	Scissors
	Acrylic paint (various colors)	Cardstock

DIRECTIONS

1. Apply a thin layer of Mod Podge to the top of the beetle. Work in sections, covering each area with glitter as you go. Let dry.

2. Paint the inside and outside of the box lid. Let dry.

3. Cut out the glittered beetle, taking extra care around any delicate parts, such as thin legs. If any part of the beetle feels fragile, use Mod Podge to attach a piece of cardstock to the back to strengthen it.

4. Fold a strip of cardstock into a small box, and attach it to the back of the beetle. This will give the beetle a three-dimensional quality when placed inside the box lid.

5. Attach the small folded box on the back of the beetle to the painted box lid using Mod Podge, and let dry.

6. Repeat this process to create an entire museum of glittery bugs!

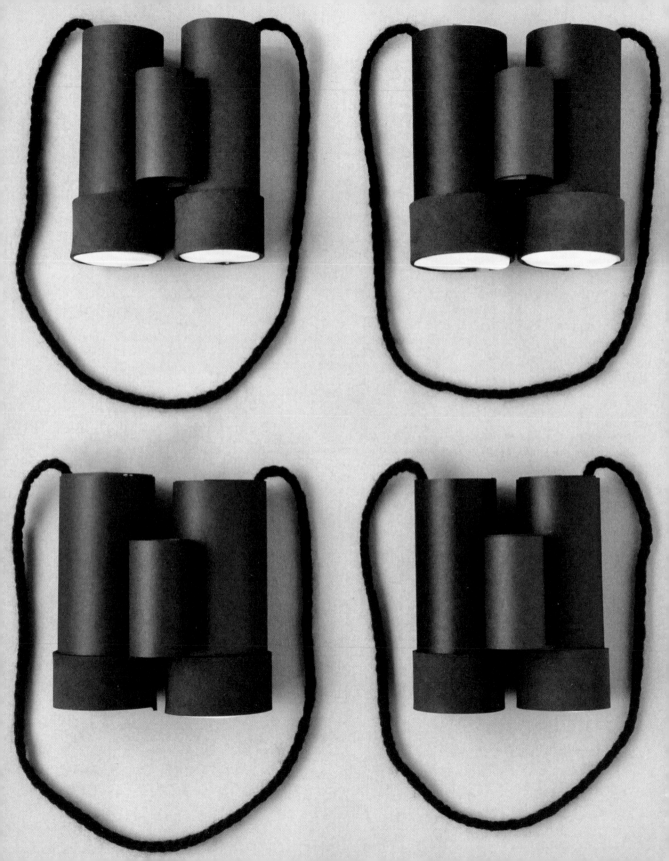

BINOCULARS

Gather empty paper rolls from around the house, and get ready to make some toys! Explore the neighborhood with this trusty pair of handmade binoculars by your side, or turn them into party favors filled with nature-themed goodies.

SUPPLIES

Scissors	Double-sided tape	Hot-glue gun and glue
Black cardstock	Pencil	Black yarn or cord
Cardboard tubes (large and small)	Craft foam (black and white)	
	Ruler	

DIRECTIONS

1. Cut black cardstock to fit around the cardboard tubes, and attach with double-sided tape. For each pair of binoculars, you will need two matching tubes, roughly the size of a toilet paper roll, and a narrower, shorter tube for the center.

2. If you want the ability to see through the binoculars instead of filling them with party favors, skip this step. Otherwise, trace the ends of the two matching rolls onto white craft foam, and cut out. Tape a circle onto the end of each tube. It's okay if the tape is visible—you will cover it later.

3. Cut black craft foam into 1-inch strips, and attach them to the end of each craft tube that has the white circles. These strips will hide any tape visible from the last step.

4. To assemble, place the two matching tubes beside each other and place the mini tube on top between them. Attach the three tubes using the hot-glue gun. Tape a piece of yarn inside each of the binocular tubes to make the neck strap.

BIRD FEEDER

Recycle an empty plastic tennis ball tube into a handmade bird feeder. Thanks to you, all the neighborhood birds will be eating in style.

Washi tape

Clear plastic tube with a lid
(from tennis balls, badminton
birdies, or similar)

Paintbrush

Outdoor acrylic paint

Black permanent marker

Ice-pop stick (jumbo)

Craft knife

Precision scissors

String

Birdseed

DIRECTIONS

1. Start by taping off a striped pattern on the plastic tube.

2. Apply a coat of outdoor acrylic paint, and let dry completely.

TIP

* The lid should fit tightly on the tube, so no glue is needed to keep it in place. If yours doesn't feel secure, use strong glue to attach the lid to the tube so you don't lose all the birdseed out the bottom.

3. Once dry, carefully remove the tape.

4. Use a permanent marker to mark a line as wide as your ice-pop stick onto one side of the tube. Keep this close to the bottom of the bird feeder, since it will be gravity fed. Use the craft knife and precision scissors to cut out the slot, making sure the ice-pop stick fits through. Then mark a line directly across from this first one so that the ice-pop stick will stick out from each side of the tube.

5. Cut a short triangle above the slot. This will allow the birdseed to slowly pour onto both ends of the ice-pop stick for the birds to eat and peck.

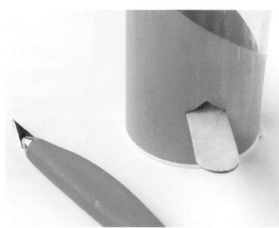

6. If your container doesn't have a hole in the top lid, use a drill to make a small hole. Cut a piece of string, and thread it through the hole in the top lid to form a loop for hanging. Fill the container with birdseed, put on the lid, and hang!

BUMBLEBEE SLIME BOXES

Nothing beats homemade slime, but it isn't the cutest thing around.
Dress it up in sweet little bumblebee containers for the coolest
party favors ever. Bee ready for some serious fun!

SUPPLIES

For the Bumblebee Boxes

Pencil

Small round containers/boxes

Yellow and black cardstock

Scissors

Mod Podge brush

Mod Podge

White vellum or
glittered paper

Small hole punch

Brads

For the Honey Slime
(makes enough to fill
4 Bumblebee Boxes)

1 cup warm water

1 tablespoon borax

½ cup Mod Podge matte

Yellow acrylic paint

Yellow glitter

DIRECTIONS

FOR THE BUMBLEBEE BOXES

1. Trace the lid of the round container/box onto yellow cardstock. Cut out one circle per favor. Cut strips of black cardstock in various widths, and attach them to the yellow circles with Mod Podge. Trim overhanging stripes to make neat, striped circles to use for the bees' bodies.

2. Using black cardstock, cut out small triangles for the bees' stingers, half-circles for the bees' heads, and small antennae.

3. Trace the lid onto vellum or glittered paper. Cut out one circle per favor. Cut the circle in half to make the bees' wings. Place the wings on each circle, overlapping them slightly on one end. Punch a hole through the overlapping layers of the wings and body. Fasten all layers together with a brad.

4. Use Mod Podge to attach the head, stinger, and antennae to the body of each bee.

FOR THE HONEY SLIME

1. In a medium bowl, mix the water and borax, stirring well until dissolved.

2. In a larger bowl, mix Mod Podge Matte and a few drops of yellow acrylic paint. Stir until fully blended.

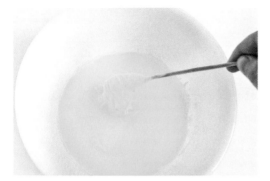 

3. Pour the borax mixture into the Mod Podge mixture, and stir. The slime should start to form. Keep stirring for about 1 minute.

4. Pour off excess water from the mixture and knead the slime with your hands for a few minutes to make sure it's thoroughly mixed and any excess water drips away. Transfer the slime to a new bowl, and mix in glitter.

TO ASSEMBLE

1. Divide the slime into your favor containers. Increase the recipe as needed if you have more containers to fill.

2. Glue the bees onto the lids of the containers, and let dry.

BUNNY CUPCAKES

You'll never make a plain cupcake again once you try your hand at these adorable bunnies. No fancy materials or cupcake toppers are required, just sprinkles and cupcake liners.

SUPPLIES

Paper cupcake liners	Baked cupcakes	Sanding sugar or sprinkles
Scissors	Frosting	Jumbo nonpareil sprinkles

DIRECTIONS

1. Cut out bunny ear shapes from the ribbed edge of the cupcake papers. Fold each ear in half (fold it against a table edge to get a sharp crease).

2. Generously frost the cupcakes. Place sanding sugar, sprinkles, or nonpareils into a bowl, and press the frosted cupcake top in the bowl to coat. Gently slide each ear into the frosting at one side of the cupcake. Place jumbo nonpareil eyes and nose on top of the cupcake.

BETTER BLONDIES

Take basic blondies to the next level by adding a few extra ingredients. Add-ins like flaky sea salt, chocolate chips, and crunchy pretzels will have everyone begging for more. Swap in other favorite add-ins such as chopped nuts, white chocolate, dried fruit, or even chopped candy bars.

— MAKES 9 BLONDIES —

INGREDIENTS

1 cup (2 sticks) unsalted butter	1¾ cups sugar	1 cup chocolate chips
2 cups flour	2 large eggs	1 cup lightly crushed pretzels, plus 16 whole pretzels for garnish
½ teaspoon flaky sea salt	1 teaspoon vanilla extract	

DIRECTIONS

1. Melt the butter in a medium saucepan over medium heat, stirring occasionally. After 5 minutes, keep a close eye on it—the butter will start to foam and brown. Remove the pan from the heat just as the butter turns golden and is very fragrant. Set aside to cool for 20 minutes.

2. Line the pan with a 1 to 2 inch overhang of parchment paper. Preheat the oven to $350°$F. Line a 9-inch square baking dish with parchment paper and butter or spray the parchment.

3. In a medium bowl, whisk together the flour and sea salt.

4. Add the sugar to the melted butter, stirring vigorously for 1 minute. Add the eggs, and stir for 2 minutes, until the mixture is smooth and shiny. Stir in the vanilla. Fold the wet ingredients into the dry, stirring until just combined. Fold in the chocolate chips and pretzels.

5. Spoon the mixture into the prepared baking dish, and smooth the top with an offset spatula. Top with the reserved pretzels and a pinch of sea salt.

6. Bake the blondies for 25 to 30 minutes. Check them at the 25-minute mark—the blondies should be just set in the center with faintly golden edges that are starting to pull away from the edge. If they're not quite ready, put them in for 2 minutes more and check again, and repeat, if needed. A shorter bake makes for a gooey center, while a longer bake makes for a cakey one.

7. Set on a wire rack to cool for 10 minutes. Use parchment to lift the blondies out of the pan, and set on the rack to cool completely. Once the blondies are cool, use a large knife to cut into 9 even squares. Blondies will keep in an airtight container at room temperature for 3 days.

CHAPTER 3

CACTUS

Don't have a green thumb? Not to worry—these pipe cleaner cacti need even less care than the real thing. Grab some pipe cleaners and pom-poms, and create a colorful collection of cacti.

SUPPLIES

Green pipe cleaners

Yarn (or store-bought pom-poms)

Scissors

Hot-glue gun and glue

DIRECTIONS

1. Shape a green pipe cleaner into a circle, twisting the ends together to secure.

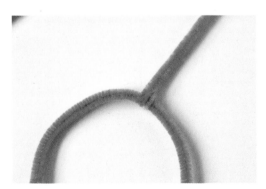

2. Attach another pipe cleaner to the circle by twisting its end around the circle and back on itself.

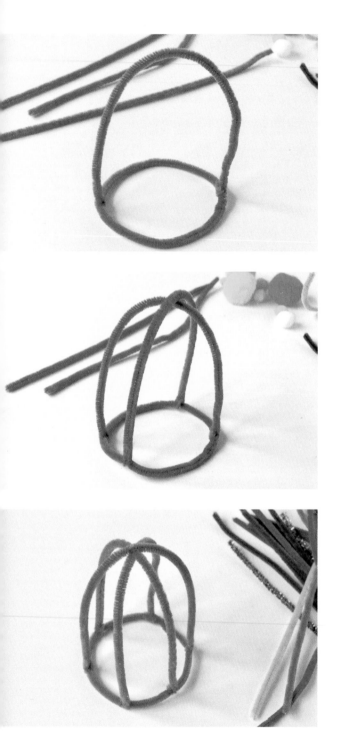

3. Link the other end of that pipe cleaner to the opposite side of the circle, forming an arch.

4. Add another pipe cleaner in the same way, positioning the arch perpendicular to the first one.

5. Twist on one more pipe cleaner. Your sculpture now looks like a simple, domed cactus.

6. To make the pom-pom flowers, wrap yarn around your four fingers 15 to 20 times. Use another piece of yarn to tie a double knot around the center. Cut the looped ends on the wrapped yarn and fluff into a pom-pom. Glue the pom-poms onto the top of the cactus. (You can use store-bought pom-poms as flowers here instead.)

TIP

* Adapt this simple technique to make cacti in different shapes. Make the base circle smaller or larger, or make the cacti taller by using two pipe cleaners connected at the ends for the arches. Make the base into a zigzag starburst shape instead of a circle and even add arms to the sides by securing them with dots of hot glue.

CALLA LILIES

Transform ordinary noodles into lovely calla lily bouquets. *Campanelle* means "bellflowers" in Italian, so it's the perfect pasta for the job. These simple steps will grow a springtime garden ready to top a cake, fill a vase, or pin on a lapel.

SUPPLIES

Dry campanelle pasta noodles

White and yellow acrylic paint

Paintbrushes

Toothpicks

Scissors

Floral stem or wire

Tacky glue

Green cardstock

DIRECTIONS

1. Paint the noodles white. Let dry.

2. Cut the toothpicks in half, paint yellow, and let dry. Glue the cut end of a yellow toothpick into the top of each noodle.

3. Cut a floral stem down to 7 to 9 inches (shorter for cupcake toppers), and poke one end through the hole in the bottom of the noodle. Add glue to secure it, if necessary.

4. Cut the leaves out of green cardstock, and fold them down the middle. Glue the end of a leaf to the stem, under the noodle. After the glue dries, gently bend the leaves away from the stem to give them more shape.

COOKIE-CUTTER CANDY POPS

These candy pops can serve as cupcake toppers, favors, or party treats. Kids will love having an excuse to play with their food! Just make sure that an adult is there to help with the iron.

Cutting board	Parchment paper (oven-safe and nonstick)	Iron and ironing board
Sharp knife	Cookie sheet	Cookie cutters
Starburst Minis		Cake pop sticks

DIRECTIONS

1. Using a sharp knife and a cutting board, cut your Starburst Minis in half diagonally to create triangles.

2. Using two different Starburst colors, squeeze two triangles together with the cut edges facing each other to make a square. You will have to mold them with your fingers a bit, but as your hands warm them, they become easier to shape. You should now have a two-toned square. Repeat this step with different color combinations, until you have enough squares to create a grid that is larger than your cookie cutter.

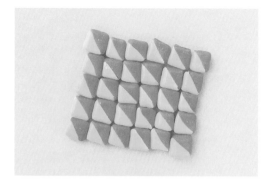

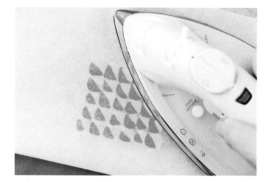

3. Place a sheet of parchment paper on a flat cookie sheet, and arrange the two-toned Starburst squares in a grid. Basically, you will place your squares in columns and rows, and make sure the pieces are touching. Remember to make it larger than your cookie cutter.

4. Preheat your iron on a low setting. Place the cookie sheet on the ironing board, and carefully cover your grid arrangement with a second sheet of parchment paper. Keeping the parchment paper between the iron and the candy, carefully iron over your grid arrangement. Do it as evenly as possible, keeping the iron level and parallel to the cookie sheet. Once the squares appear to be fairly melted together and the candy is the same thickness throughout, flip the candy grid to the other side, keeping it sandwiched between the two pieces of parchment paper on the cookie sheet. Iron the second side of your candy grid until all the pieces are sufficiently melted together.

5. Set your iron aside, and let the grid cool a bit before peeling the top sheet of parchment paper off the candy. If it peels the candy up at all, wait a few more seconds before trying again. Place your cookie cutter on the candy, and press down until it goes all the way through. Carefully peel the candy up around the sides of the cookie cutter. Once the cutter is free, use your fingers to pop out your candy shape.

6. Take the remaining candy that you peeled from the edges of the cutter and either ball it up, or carefully piece it back together, and repeat steps 4 and 5 with the "leftovers." If you have enough room, you will want to use the same cookie cutter to make your candy pop. If not, just use some smaller cookie cutters to use up the candy and create another grid to make your second piece using the same cookie cutter.

7. Once you have two identical shapes, sandwich a cake pop stick between them, lining up the shapes so that they mirror each other perfectly. Place them between the two pieces of parchment paper on the cookie sheet and carefully iron over both sides of the shape. Once it cools enough to peel off the parchment paper, use your fingers to press the pieces together while they are still warm. You may have to repeat this step one more time to seal the pieces together around the cake pop stick. Lay your candy pop on a flat surface to cool.

a b c d e f g h i j k l m

hello friend

CHARCOAL

Grab a sketchbook and have fun experimenting with these hand-made charcoal pencils. If you haven't sketched with charcoal before, try using different pressures, lines, and techniques to create different shades and looks.

SUPPLIES

Candle

Bamboo skewers
(cut into shorter pieces)

Matches

DIRECTIONS

1. Light the candle, and carefully hold one end of the bamboo skewer over the flame. Turn it slowly, watching as the skewer burns and turns black.

2. After letting it turn to charcoal, blow out the flame and let the charcoal pencil cool.

TIPS

* Ask for permission and/or supervision from an adult before using an open flame.

* Experiment with creating different shades with your charcoal pencils. If you allow them to burn longer or shorter, does the quality of the charcoal change?

CHEWY CHECKERS

This super-sweet set of checkers is a great way to have fun as a family while satisfying your sweet tooth. Just make sure you don't eat all the pieces before the game is over! Add a personal touch by putting your favorite candy on top of the rainbow fudge.

SUPPLIES

2 cups white chocolate chips	Flavoring	Plastic wrap
1 (16-ouce) tub white frosting	Striped candy in two colors	Aluminum foil (optional)
Food coloring		

DIRECTIONS

1. Put 1 cup of the white chocolate chips in a microwave-safe bowl. Melt them in the microwave in 30-second intervals, stirring after each to prevent any burning. Repeat with the remaining 1 cup white chocolate chips in a separate bowl.

2. Add about half the frosting to each bowl and stir to combine. Stir in a few drops of food coloring and flavoring, tinting one bowl pink and one bowl blue. (You will need two colors of fudge for the checkers.)

3. Cut the candy strips into squares—you'll need 12 of each color.

4. Line a 9-inch square pan with plastic wrap, and put the pink fudge in one half and the blue fudge in the other half, using a piece of aluminum foil as a barrier between them. (If you have two loaf pans, you can use these to save a few minutes; just put one color of fudge in each pan.) Place the candy squares onto the fudge in a grid, and then refrigerate, covered, to chill for at least 30 minutes.

5. Once the fudge hardens, use a sharp knife to cut it into pieces around the candy squares. Leave as is, or put into mini muffin cups to serve or play checkers with. Use on a regular checkerboard or make your own out of cardstock and clear contact paper so that it can be wiped off.

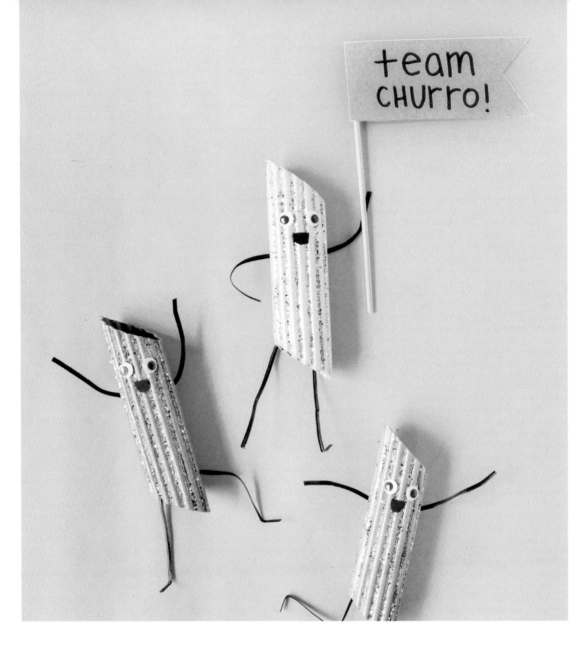

CHURRO ACTION FIGURES

On a scale from 1 to 10, how much do you love churros? Celebrate this sweet dessert by turning it into action figures. Penne, manicotti, and other ridged pasta look a lot like churros, so you can make these in almost any size.

Dry, ridged pasta shapes	Gold glitter	Googly eyes
Paintbrushes	Black cardstock	Black wire
Multisurface acrylic paint	Scissors	
Mod Podge	Hot-glue gun and glue	

DIRECTIONS

1. Paint the noodles brown (use a few different shades for variety), and allow to dry.

2. Apply a coat of Mod Podge to the noodles, and sprinkle with glitter. Let dry.

3. Cut small mouths out of black cardstock, and hot glue them onto the noodles. Glue 2 googly eyes onto each as well.

4. Cut pieces of black wire into arms and legs, and hot glue them onto the backs of the churros.

CUCUMBER CAKES

Who says cake has to be sweet? These colorful cucumbers are celebration-ready, and an exciting way to add some vegetables to the menu at your next party.

INGREDIENTS

Cucumbers	Radishes
Carrots	Cream cheese

DIRECTIONS

1. Wash the cucumbers, and slice into ½-inch-thick rounds.

2. For sprinkles, shred the carrots and radishes using a grater, or use a knife and cutting board to carefully cut them into stripes or circles.

3. Put the cream cheese in a plastic bag and cut off one corner, making a piping bag. Gently squeeze the bag, applying the cream cheese onto a cucumber slice. Place another slice on top, and apply more cream cheese. Each cake should have two or three cucumber slice layers.

4. Apply more cream cheese on top of the cucumber cake. Sprinkle with carrot and radish sprinkles, or arrange them in a pattern.

CHAPTER 4

DAFFODIL CUPCAKES

Embrace flowers and your sweet tooth all at once with these tasty daffodil cupcake toppers. They make a perfect dessert for Easter, Mother's Day, or any springtime occasion.

SUPPLIES

Baked cupcakes

Green frosting

Airheads candies
(yellow and white)

Citrus slice candies
(yellow and orange)

Scissors

DIRECTIONS

1. Use scissors to cut the Airheads into petal shapes. Each flower needs 6 petals.

2. Frost the baked cupcakes with green frosting, and arrange 6 petals evenly on each. Place 2 citrus slice candies on top to form the center of each.

TIP

* For the paler yellow petals, we used banana marshmallow candies. Flatten the candies with a rolling pin, and cut off the ends if they are too long to fit on the cupcake.

DIORAMAS

Not a fan of sardines? This project might get you to give them another try. Check the canned fish aisle at your local supermarket to find a handful of different-shaped cans to use for these dioramas. Felt, paint, and a little imagination will give the cans a new life as miniature works of art.

SUPPLIES

Assorted empty
sardine cans

Felt scraps

Multisurface acrylic paint

Paintbrushes

Glue

Scissors

Pom-poms

Small plastic animals

An assortment of craft
supplies for details

DIRECTIONS

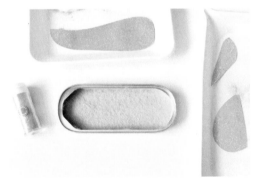

1. Thoroughly wash and dry the sardine cans. Cut a piece of felt, and glue it inside the can to use as a background for the diorama. You can also use paper or paint to create a more detailed background.

2. To create the desert diorama, cut assorted colors of cardstock into hills of sand and cover with glitter. Let dry, and then glue inside the can. To finish the scene, add a small plastic animal or toy, like the pink camel pictured.

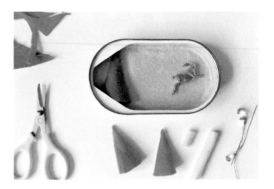

3. To create the jungle diorama, cut green cardstock into tropical leaves, and glue them inside the can. Place a small object in the middle, like the yellow lion pictured, and add a few blades of grass cut from green cardstock to add depth.

4. To create the forest diorama, make three small evergreen trees from felt, and glue them in place. Place a few miniature toadstools and felt blades of grass next to the trees. Attach a small plastic animal or figure to finish the scene.

5. To create the wild blueberry diorama, use pipe cleaners to make the stem of the plant. Add leaves made from cardstock covered in green glitter to the stem. Cut tiny circles of contrasting blue felt, and glue them onto pom-poms to make the blueberries. Attach the blueberries to the pipe cleaner stem.

6. To create the caterpillar diorama, cut and fold cardstock leaves and glue them inside the can. Glue pom-poms together to make the body of the caterpillar. Add two pieces of string for the antenna, and draw the face with a fine-tip marker. Glue the caterpillar to a leaf inside the can.

DIVER PUPPET

This puppet is sure to make a big splash. Using just a few materials, you'll be ready for a deep-sea adventure. If you're lucky, you may even find sunken treasure or hidden gold.

5 small round wooden beads

Paper drinking straws
(regular and jumbo)

Toilet paper tube

Multisurface acrylic paint

Paintbrush

Pipe cleaners

1 large wooden bead

White cardstock

Hot-glue gun and glue

String

Wooden dowel

DIRECTIONS

1. Paint 4 of the small wooden beads, 4 regular paper straws, and the toilet paper tube with black paint. Let dry.

2. Cut the straws into 8 equal pieces, about 1¾ inches long each, and a longer piece about 4 inches long. Fold 3 black pipe cleaners in half, and thread the straws and beads onto each as shown, forming the diver's arms, legs, and torso.

3. Paint the large wooden bead with black paint to look like a diver's face. Let dry.

4. To make the diver's accessories, cut a jumbo paper straw into 2 pieces, about 2 inches long each. Paint the paper straws, 1 small round bead, and a piece of white cardstock with yellow paint. Once dry, cut the now yellow cardstock into two flippers.

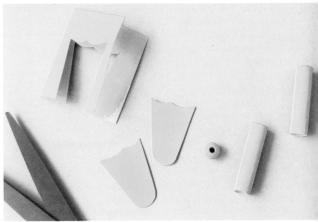

5. Assemble the diver by twisting the torso pipe cleaner onto the arms and legs. Hot glue the head onto an extra pipe cleaner that extends out past the torso. Twist the pipe cleaners on the arms and legs into small loops to be hands and feet.

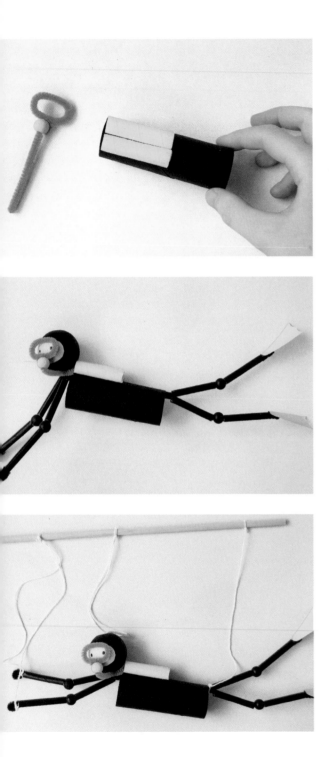

6. Cut the black tube so that it's 4 inches long. Cut it open along its length, then reroll it so it's narrower, and glue it closed again. Hot glue the two yellow straws onto the back as the oxygen supply. Bend and twist a green pipe cleaner into an oblong loop, and thread the yellow bead up next to the loop.

7. Place the black tube over the torso straw, hot gluing it to secure. Hot glue the pipe cleaner mask onto the face, and bend the excess pipe cleaner to connect it to the air supply.

8. Cut and tie pieces of string onto the diver's arms, head, and hips, and tie the ends of the strings to a wooden dowel.

DONUT BUNNIES

Public service announcement: Bunnies aren't just for Easter. Decorating donuts to look like cute rabbits couldn't be easier. And if you use store-bought donut holes, you won't even have to turn on your oven.

Chocolate melting wafers (pink and white)	Donut holes	Scissors
	Spoon	Paper muffin liners
Bowls	Black icing gel	
Wire rack	Toothpicks	

DIRECTIONS

1. Put the pink chocolate melting wafers in a microwave-safe bowl, and melt them in the microwave in 15-second intervals, stirring after each. Repeat with the white chocolate melting wafers in a separate bowl. In separate small bowls, mix the pink and white chocolate to create different shades of pink.

2. Set a wire rack over a baking sheet. Dip the donut holes into the melted chocolate to coat them completely, and use a spoon to tidy up or smooth any messy blobs. Put the coated donut holes on the wire rack to set.

3. Use a contrasting pink to make a small circle for the bunny's mouth and nose area. Let dry. Use the black icing gel and a toothpick to draw on a nose and mouth, and then eyes.

4. Cut the muffin liners into 1-inch-tall ears, creasing them down the center to help them stand up better. Use a toothpick to make a little slot in the icing and insert the ears.

CHAPTER 5

EGG PARTY FAVORS

Make these sunny-side-up eggs to decorate your kitchen table for brunch. They can be used individually as place settings or arranged as a group down the middle of the table. Your friends will enjoy finding a surprise hidden under each yolk.

SUPPLIES

Cutting mat	Gesso primer	White cardstock
Ping-Pong balls	Paintbrushes	Scissors
Craft knife	Multisurface acrylic paint	

DIRECTIONS

1. Carefully cut the Ping-Pong balls in half using a craft knife, following the seam. Each half is one yolk.

2. Use gesso primer to paint the yolks. Let dry.

3. Paint pastel colors on each yolk. Let dry.

4. Cut a curved "blob" shape out of white cardstock to be the egg white.

5. To assemble each "egg," place the egg white on the table, top it with a few treats, and hide them under the yolk.

EASY EMBROIDERY

If you have little ones who are just learning to sew, pipe cleaner embroidery is the perfect way to get them started. A needle and thread can be a little bit tricky for kids new to sewing, but pipe cleaners are easy to handle and thread through plastic embroidery canvas.

| Plastic embroidery canvas | : | Pipe cleaners | : | Safety pins (optional) |
| Scissors | : | Beads | : | |

DIRECTIONS

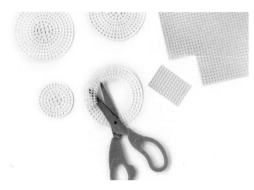

1. Cut the plastic embroidery canvas into whatever shape you like. If using a large rectangle, trim off a smaller square or rectangle. If using small circular canvases, leave them as is or trim off a few of the outer rows to make a smaller circle.

2. Pick a pipe cleaner, and think about what design you want to make. Faces are a good place to start. To make a smiling mouth, thread one end of the pipe cleaner into the grid, bending a tiny little tail back on itself on the back of the canvas to lock it in place. Curve the pipe cleaner into a smile shape and thread it into another square on the grid, pulling it through so that the pipe cleaner smile sits flat against the canvas in the shape that you want. Trim the excess, leaving a small tail, and then fold the tail back on itself on the back of the canvas to secure the smile.

3. To make the eyes, cut a piece of pipe cleaner about 1½ inches long, and thread it through a bead. Then thread both ends of the pipe cleaner through the canvas, and twist them together at the back. Add a second eye in the same way.

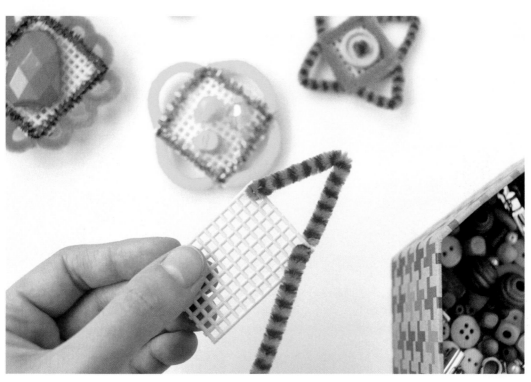

4. You can also make abstract badge-inspired embroidery. Use your beads as inspiration, and add pipe cleaner borders and edges. When complete, hook a safety pin through the top, and pin them onto your child's backpack as fun little charms!

ENVELOPES

Is there anything better than getting a letter in the mail? These colorful envelopes are a great way to reuse old paper scraps and re-purpose old envelopes. Enclose special notes to mail to family and friends, or store your favorite stickers, notes, and confetti inside.

SUPPLIES

Empty used envelopes	Pencil	Mod Podge
Scrap paper (magazines, wrapping paper, poster board, etc.)	Scissors	Mod Podge brush

DIRECTIONS

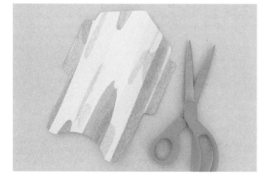 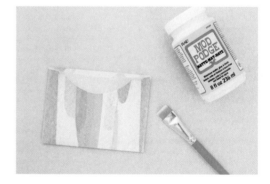

1. Carefully unfold an envelope, and lay it flat onto a piece of scrap paper. Trace around the outside with a pencil, and cut out the shape.

2. Fold the paper to mimic the folds on the original envelope. Use Mod Podge to attach the flaps in place. Make sure to leave the top fold open for now.

3. Fill the envelope with notes, poems, and songs! Decorate the front with make-believe stamps and addresses.

ERASER PIÑATA

Celebrate school and lifelong learning with a favorite school supply crafted into a piñata. The pink eraser is a classic. Because of its simple shape, it's easy to make.

Cardboard	Masking tape	Black cardstock (or alphabet stickers)
Craft knife	Pink crepe paper	Paper-cutting machine (optional)
Pencil	String	
Ruler	Packing tape	White glue
Scissors		

DIRECTIONS

1. Cut two 11 by 19-inch rectangles and two 6 by 11-inch rectangles out of cardboard.

2. Use masking tape to attach the four rectangles to form a sort of rectangular tube. Adjust the shape into the parallelogram shape (think "angled rectangle") of a classic Pink Pearl eraser, and tape to secure.

3. Trace the parallelogram shape onto cardboard and cut out two of them.

4. Tape one of the solid parallelogram pieces to the bottom of the open parallelogram, and then fill with back-to-school supplies and treats! Tape the remaining solid parallelogram piece to the top to close the piñata.

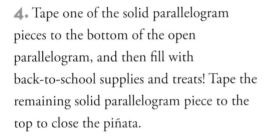

5. Cut 1-inch-wide pieces of the pink crepe paper, and fringe one side of each. Use white glue to apply the fringed crepe paper to the piñata, starting at the bottom and working your way up until you've covered all sides. Before you cover the top, use packing tape to securely attach a piece of string for hanging the piñata.

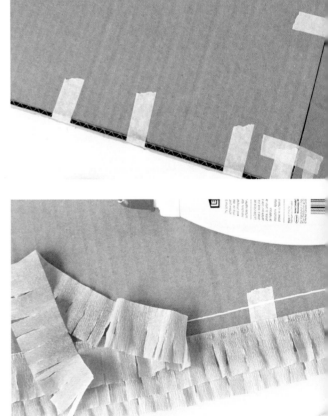

6. Use a paper-cutting machine (or pencil and scissors) to draw and cut the classic Pink Pearl logo out of black cardstock. Place the logo onto the piñata, and use white glue to attach.

CHAPTER 6

FINGERPRINT PUMPKINS

Fingerprint art is a foolproof way to make memories with your little ones. You can fingerprint almost anything and instantly turn it into a keepsake or handmade gift for friends and family. Pumpkins, dishes, frames . . . make fingerprint art on all of it!

SUPPLIES

Multisurface acrylic paint

Paper plate

White pumpkin

Fine paintbrushes

DIRECTIONS

1. Pour some paint onto the paper plate and dip your thumb (or another finger) into the paint. Practice with a few thumbprint stamps on the paper plate first to see how much paint you need for the best print. For the pineapple pattern, stamp the thumbprints vertically all over the pumpkin.

2. To add leaf detail to the pineapple, use a fine paintbrush and green paint. Simply paint three small wisps at the top of each thumbprint.

3. Use a fine paintbrush to paint tiny black dots on the thumbprint for the pineapple texture. (You can use a black marker to make the dots instead.)

4. The steps are essentially the same for the jack-o'-lantern and cacti pumpkins. For the jack-o'-lantern, use orange paint and sideways thumbprints. Paint the stem details with green paint and the faces with black paint. For the cacti pumpkin, use green paint and vertical thumbprints (some solo, some stacked in twos or threes) and then add black "spiky" details and colorful flowers at the tops.

FLOWER PAPER CLIPS

Staying organized is so much more fun when you have cute accessories. Flower clips are quick and easy to make, and you can decorate them in so many ways. They're perfect for clipping onto your notebook or calendar, and they also make great gifts for the stationery-loving people in your life.

Pencil	Scissors	White glue
Freezer paper	Felt	Jumbo paper clips (green, if possible)
Iron and Ironing boad	Multisurface acrylic paint	
	Paintbrush	

DIRECTIONS

1. Trace flower and leaf shapes on the paper side (the dull side) of the freezer paper. For each clip, you need two matching shapes for the flower and leaf. To make it easier, group the shapes by color and then cut the groups apart. With the shiny side down, iron the freezer paper to the felt.

2. Cut out the shapes using the traced freezer paper lines as a guide. Peel the paper off the felt.

3. Decorate the flower pieces with paint. You can paint both the front and the back of each flower shape or just the front. If you decorate both, make sure to paint the right sides of the felt so they still match up with the unpainted sides touching. Let dry.

4. Apply glue around the edge of the back piece of the flower. Add a little extra to the middle. Press the end of the jumbo paper clip with just one loop into the glue as shown. Place the front flower piece on top.

5. Slip one end of a leaf piece between the clip side of the paper clip as shown. Push it up halfway and angle it however you like. Apply glue to the felt leaf, covering the paper clip. Gently press the second leaf piece onto the glue. Let dry.

FORTUNE COOKIES

Turn everyone's favorite cookie into a paper treat that will last forever. These come together quickly, so it's easy to make an entire batch to use as party favors or as a fun take on Christmas crackers.

SUPPLIES

5-inch bowl	Scissors	Stickers
Colored paper	Stamps	Hot-glue gun and glue
Pencil	Ink pad	

DIRECTIONS

1. Find a bowl that's about 5 inches in diameter. Turn it upside down on a sheet of colored paper, and trace it.

2. Cut out the circles.

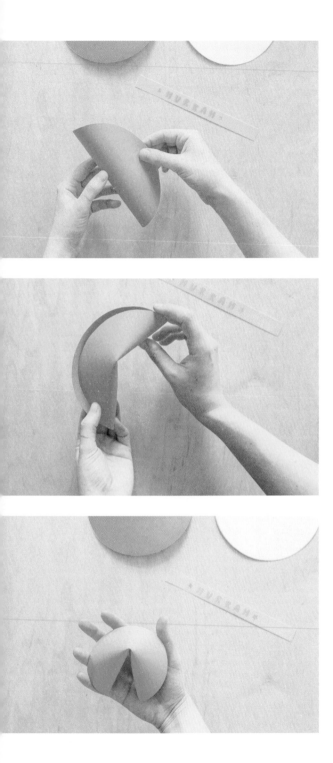

3. Gently fold the circle in half, without creasing the paper.

4. Gently pinch the two ends of the half-circle together.

5. The paper should now look like a fortune cookie with a gentle crease in the middle. Set aside for now. Don't worry if the fortune cookie unfolds; it will be glued in place later.

6. Cut strips of paper and use stamps and an ink pad to write out happy messages and fortunes.

7. Gently reshape the fortune cookie, and slide the paper strip into it. Apply a dot of hot glue onto the fortune cookie above the crease and press the two sides together so that the fortune stays in place and the cookie doesn't pop open.

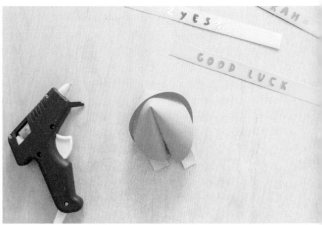

FRIENDSHIP BRACELETS

Did you know that you can weave with drinking straws? Gather up some colorful yarn and grab some paper straws to make these woven yarn friendship bracelets. They're fun to make and the possibilities are endless.

SUPPLIES

Drinking straws	Colored yarn	White glue
Scissors	Washi tape	Sequins

DIRECTIONS

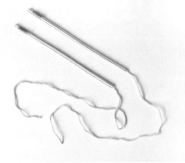 

1. Cut a short snip into one end of a drinking straw. Feed a piece of yarn through the straw, pull the end of the yarn into the slit, and wrap it with a piece of washi tape to secure it in place. Leave about 12 inches of yarn extended past the opposite end of the straw. Repeat with a second straw.

2. Take another piece of yarn (leave it attached to the ball for now) in one hand, and hold the two straws with your other hand. Wrap the yarn around one straw, then the other, making a figure eight as you weave around them, as shown.

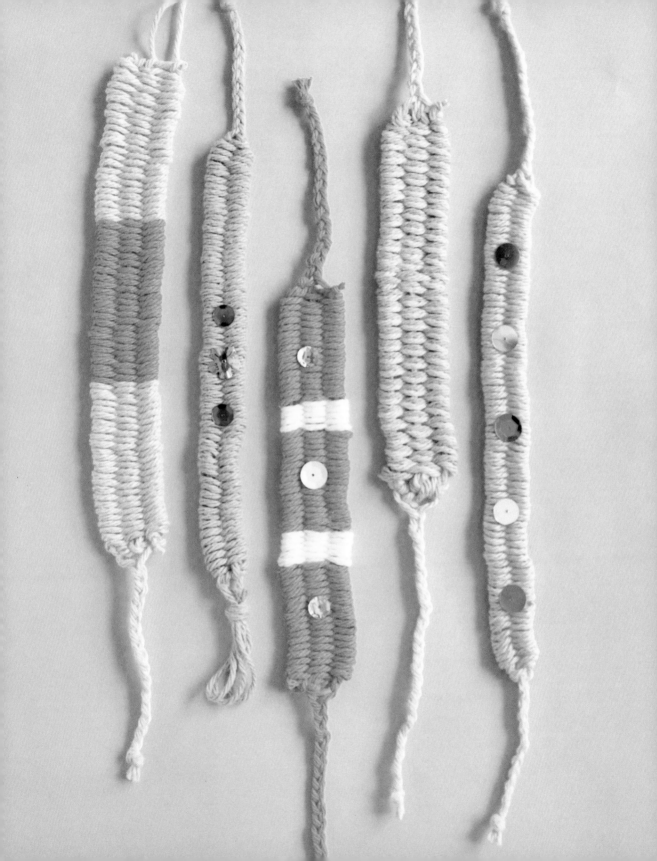

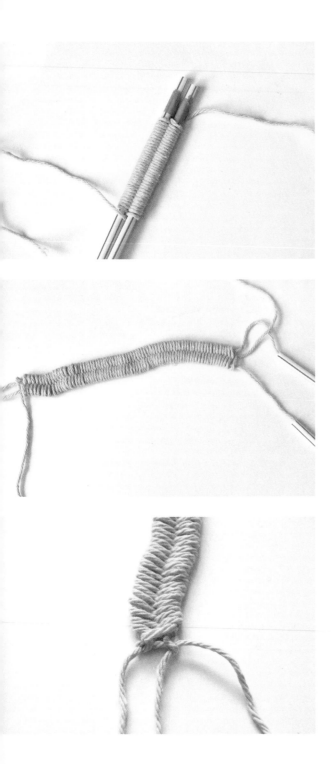

3. Keep wrapping the yarn around the straws, sliding the yarn down the straws as you go.

4. When you are happy with the length of your bracelet, slide it off the straws. Cut the vertical yarns so that the bracelet is free from the straws.

5. Use the excess length of the wrapping yarn to tie double knots onto each of the vertical yarns on each end.

6. Braid the three tails together, or tie a loop, depending on how you would like to wear the bracelet.

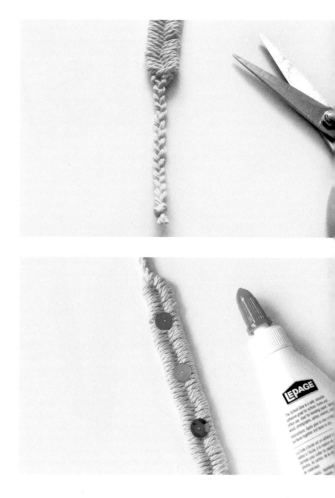

7. Use white glue to attach sequins or beads for extra decoration. Repeat to make bracelets for all your friends.

TIPS

* Try using more straws or straws of different sizes, or weave two pieces of yarn at once!

* You can also make stripes by switching colors. Just tie a new color of yarn onto the one you started weaving with and switch back and forth as you like.

FLAMINGOS

Dress up your front lawn using painted gourds. These are big ball dipper gourds, but if your local farm has swan gourds, those will work nicely, too. Adding playful quirkiness to your neighborhood has never been more fun.

SUPPLIES

Multisurface acrylic paint	Waterproof Mod Podge (optional)	White glue or double-sided tape
Paintbrushes	Wooden dowels	Scissors
Swan gourds	Drill	Pink cardstock

DIRECTIONS

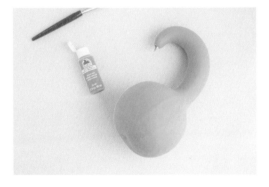

1. Paint the gourds pink. Let dry. If you plan on keeping your flamingos outside during rainy weather, apply a coat of waterproof Mod Podge.

2. Paint the beak and eye details using black paint.

3. Paint the dowels pink. You can leave a small section on one end unpainted so you can hold while painting—it will be hidden later. Let dry.

4. Drill two holes the size of your dowels into the bottom of the flamingos.

5. Insert the painted dowels into the drilled holes.

6. Cut out paper wings from pink cardstock, and use white glue or double-sided tape to attach to the painted flamingos. If you plan on keeping the flamingos outside for a few days in potentially rainy weather, you might want to skip this step. The pink gourds still look like flamingos at this step, without the paper wings. If you plan to keep the flamingos inside as decorations in potted plants, under an overhang at your front door, or you are lucky enough to have no rain in the forecast, you should be safe! Stick the flamingos in the grass.

FANCY FRENCH TOAST

There's nothing better than waking up to the smell of French toast in the morning! This recipe brings a citrus twist that is sure to brighten even the dreariest of days. Golden brown toast brings nostalgia of the classic dish, while bursts of orange flavor add a surprise for your taste buds. Experiment with different types of oranges to perfect the flavor—navel, blood, and Cara Cara oranges are all excellent options.

— SERVES 4 —

INGREDIENTS

For the syrup

½ cup maple syrup

1 cup orange segments (use a mix of tangerine, navel, and blood oranges)

For the French toast

5 large eggs

Zest of 1 orange

½ cup fresh orange juice (from about 2 oranges)

1 cup whole milk

1 tablespoon granulated sugar

½ teaspoon sea salt

1 teaspoon pure vanilla extract

8 thick-cut slices brioche

3 tablespoons unsalted butter, for frying

For serving

Confectioners' sugar

Orange slices (optional)

DIRECTIONS

1. Slide a rimmed baking sheet into the oven, and preheat the oven to 200°F.

2. To make the syrup, in a nonreactive medium saucepan, combine the maple syrup and orange segments, and heat over medium heat. When the mixture just begins to bubble, remove from the heat and set aside to cool.

3. To make the French toast, in a large bowl, whisk together the eggs, orange zest, orange juice, milk, granulated sugar, salt, and vanilla.

4. Heat a large skillet over medium to medium-high heat. When the pan is hot, add 2 tablespoons butter, and let it melt. Dip 3 or 4 slices of bread in the batter, immerse them briefly to coat, and then use a slotted spatula to transfer the bread to the hot skillet. Cook until golden on the bottom, 2 to 4 minutes, and then flip and cook on the second side for 2 to 4 minutes. Transfer the cooked French toast to the warm pan in the oven. Repeat with the remaining bread, adding more butter to the skillet as needed.

5. To serve, dust the French toast with confectioners' sugar, and top with the orange maple syrup. If desired, garnish with fresh citrus slices.

CHAPTER 7

GRADUATION OWLS

These wise owls are almost too cute to eat. Dip your own chocolate pretzels using any color of chocolate and use them to dress up store-bought cupcakes. The owls are great for any school-related event, but they're especially perfect for graduations.

SUPPLIES

Chocolate melting wafers (white, pink, red)

Fork

Large pretzels

Spoons

Baked cupcakes

Frosting

Assorted sprinkles and jimmies

Toothpick

Sharp knife

Cutting board

Foil-wrapped chocolate cups

Parchment paper

DIRECTIONS

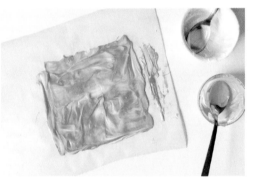

1. Melt some chocolate in the microwave, and use a fork to dip the pretzels into the melted chocolate. Let the excess drip off, and then place the dipped pretzels on parchment paper to harden completely.

2. Melt some pink chocolate, and spread it into a thin layer on a separate piece of parchment paper. The pink is used for the beaks, so you don't need too much. Let harden completely. Do the same for the red chocolate melting wafers, but melt more—this is used for the tops of the graduation hats.

3. Frost the cupcakes, keeping the surface of the frosting as smooth as possible.

4. Place a chocolate-covered pretzel onto each cupcake, toward the bottom to leave room for the hat on top as shown. Fill the middle section of the pretzel with sugar sprinkles.

5. For the eyes, place round sprinkles in the other two sections of the pretzel. For some, we used both flat and round sprinkles, but on others, we used only large round ones. Have fun mixing it up!

6. Melt a small amount of chocolate (in a color to match the pretzel), and use a toothpick to apply a small line above the eyes. Place pink jimmies on the melted chocolate to form eyebrows.

7. Cut the foil-wrapped chocolate cup in half for the graduation cap. Next, cut a red chocolate triangle about 2 inches across on the base and 1¼ inches tall for the top of the cap. Finally, cut a small pink triangle for the beak about ½ inch tall.

8. Use a small dab of melted chocolate to secure the beak onto the pretzel. Place the half foil cup above the pretzel and put a small amount of melted chocolate on the very top of the foil cup. Place the red chocolate triangle above the foil cup, gently pressing to adhere. Place next to a cup or jar for support until hardened, if necessary.

GUMDROP SWANS

Transform gumdrops into playful yet serene swans. They're also tasty—on their own or used to decorate a cake. Playing with your food is encouraged when these swans are around.

SUPPLIES

White gumdrops
(2 per swan)

Cutting board

Knife

Orange gumdrop

DIRECTIONS

1. Lay a white gumdrop on its side and use a knife to make a cut (the long way) between the middle and edge of the gumdrop. Make an identical cut on the other side of the gumdrop. These two outer pieces are the wings. Save the middle piece for later.

2. Cut about four slits in each wing from the wide end toward the narrow end to almost the middle of the wing pieces.

3. Fan out the wings and attach them to a new white gumdrop with the narrow ends of the wings touching the narrow end of the gumdrop. They are sticky enough to attach with a little pressure.

4. Lay the remaining middle piece of white gumdrop flat, and cut a fairly skinny piece off the long side. There will be a sugary side and a sticky gummy side. Next, cut an even skinnier piece off the remaining long side. This piece will be completely sticky.

5. Roll the sticky piece up from one end like a sleeping bag until it is stuck together in a small white ball.

6. Attach the ball to the top of the skinny-cut piece to look like a head and neck. It is easiest to attach the head using the edge of the rolled end and the sticky side of the "neck" piece.

7. Cut off a tiny piece of your orange gumdrop, and trim it into a triangular shape. Hold it up to the swan to check the size, and when you are satisfied with the proportions, attach the beak by sticking it to the front and middle of the head.

8. Attach the neck with the head to the front of the body, right between the wings. Push the pieces together until they stick.

GRANOLA BARS

A granola bar that feels like a brownie, these chewy chocolate granola bars are an excellent cure for afternoon cravings. They're also portable enough to be just right for breakfast on the run or a quick lunchbox treat.

— MAKES SIXTEEN 2-INCH BARS —

INGREDIENTS

2 cups rolled oats	1/4 cup unsweetened cocoa powder	1 cup unsweetened applesauce
1/2 cup raw hulled pumpkin seeds	1 teaspoon ground cinnamon	1/2 cup honey
1/2 cup raw hulled sunflower seeds	1/4 teaspoon ground allspice	1 cup sweetened dried cranberries
1/4 cup chia seeds	1/2 teaspoon sea salt	1/2 cup chocolate chips

DIRECTIONS

1. Preheat the oven to 350°F. Line an 8-inch square baking pan with parchment.

2. In a food processor, combine the oats, pumpkin, sunflower, and chia seeds, and pulse twice, just enough to break up the ingredients a bit.

3. Spoon into a large bowl, and stir in the cocoa powder, cinnamon, allspice, salt, applesauce, and honey. Fold in the cranberries and chocolate chips, reserving 2 tablespoons of the chocolate chips for the top. Press the mixture into the prepared baking pan. Press the reserved 2 tablespoons chocolate chips flat-side up into the top.

4. Bake for 30 to 40 minutes, until the granola is set in the middle and beginning to pull away from the sides of the pan. Let cool completely in the pan before cutting into squares, at least 4 hours. Cut into 16 squares, and store in an airtight container in the fridge for up to 4 days.

CHAPTER 8

HAIR CHARMS

Give yourself a little extra luck with giant charm hair clips. Wear them all at once, or spread the luck around by giving them out as party favors or small handmade gifts.

SUPPLIES

Parchment paper	Gloves (optional)	Scissors
Crayola Model Magic	Pencil	Tape
Food coloring	Scrap paper	Bobby pins

DIRECTIONS

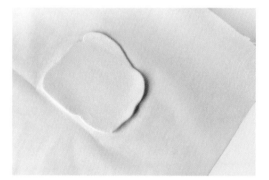

1. Lay a piece of parchment paper on your work surface. Grab a handful of Model Magic, and add food coloring to change the color—wear gloves if you don't want your hands to be dyed. Roll out flat until about ¼ inch thick.

2. Draw Lucky Charms shapes (hearts, stars, horseshoes, four-leaf clovers, blue moons, rainbows, hourglasses, and red balloons), about 2 inches tall, onto paper, and cut them out.

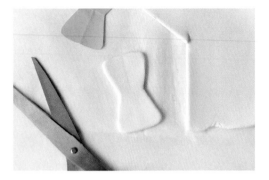

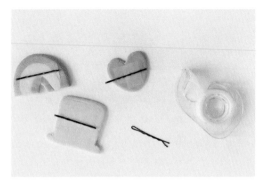

3. Place your paper pattern onto the rolled Model Magic, and use scissors to cut out the shape. The Model Magic is just tacky enough to hold the paper in place as you cut. Repeat for all the shapes, and let dry.

4. Use tape to attach a bobby pin onto the back of each Lucky Charm. The tape should be strong enough to last the day, but if you want something more permanent, use a short piece of ribbon and glue instead.

HALF MILKS

Kids will love creating these sweet science experiments in the kitchen. Candy, berries, syrup, and juice are all great add-ins to try mixing with milk. Get out all the glasses in your cupboard—it won't be long before you have a whole menu of half milks ready for sampling.

½ glass milk	Paper	Suggested add-ins
½ glass add-ins of your choice (see the suggested add-ins for ideas!)	Scissors	Juice
	Tape	Honey
Drinking glass		Berries and fruit
		Candies

DIRECTIONS

1. Pour milk into a drinking glass so that it's half full.
2. Add a variety of delicious ingredients, picking whatever you like best.
3. Decorate the outside of your glass, too. What crazy milk creations will you mix up?
4. Enjoy your milk!

HAPPY MAIL PENCIL CASE

Make this handmade pencil case, and you'll find happy mail filled with pens and pencils every time you open your backpack. With a bit of hand embroidery and some very simple sewing, you can create and customize an envelope all your own.

Iron and ironing board

9 by 12-inch piece of fusible interfacing

2-inch square piece of paper-backed fusible web

2 by 2-inch piece of cotton fabric with a cute design

Scissors

9 by 12-inch piece of linen

9 by 12-inch piece of cotton fabric

8½ by 11-inch piece of paper

Pencil

Ruler

1-inch square piece of black or dark gray felt

Happy mail template (visit hcbook.com/templates for a printable template)

Sewing needle

Embroidery floss

Pins

Sewing machine

Hammer

Hammer-on snap

Pinking shears

DIRECTIONS

1. Iron the interfacing onto the back of the linen fabric, following the instructions on the interfacing packaging.

2. Iron the fusible web on the back of the small piece of cotton fabric so it's centered behind the design you want for the stamp.

3. Cut down the linen and cotton fabric to 8½ by 11 inches (use a sheet of US letter-size paper as a guide). On each piece, mark the center of the top and each side 2½ inches down from the top. Use a ruler to make a line from the center to each of the side markings, and then trim off the corners. Each piece should now look like a house shape.

4. Cut out two ½-inch round eyes from felt. Cut the stamp from the small piece of cotton fabric so that it is approximately 1-inch square. The size can be adjusted to best fit your fabric's design, and you can have the stamp turned in either direction depending on your fabric. Refer to the printable template at hcbook.com/templates if needed.

5. Fold up the bottom edge of the linen to the bottom of the triangle flap section, and lightly crease it. Fold down the triangle flap, and lightly crease it. Draw the face and a postmark onto the center section of the envelope. The postmark is made up of a ¾-inch circle with three 1-inch wavy lines to the left. Make the edge of the postmark at least ¾ inch from the right edge. (A template that can be printed and traced to make this step even easier is available at hcbook.com/templates.)

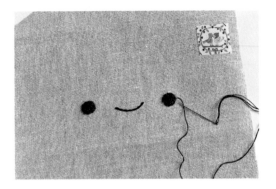

6. Peel the paper backing off the stamp, and iron it in place in the top corner of the center section of the envelope. It should be at least ½ inch from the edge. The stamp may cover part of the postmark tracing, but you can redraw that so it's pretty close to the pattern.

7. Stitch the mouth with six strands of black embroidery floss and back stitch. Attach the eyes with two strands of black embroidery floss and tiny whip stitches around the edge. Add white French knots for a highlight.

8. Stitch around the edge of the stamp with three strands of coordinating embroidery floss and back stitch. Use three strands of red embroidery floss and back stitch for the postmark. If you want to customize it, add initials in the center of the postmark!

9. Pin the two shaped fabric pieces with the wrong sides together. Sew around the entire shape with matching thread about ¼ inch from the edge.

10. Fold the envelope pieces again, and attach one half of the snap to the flap and the other half to the back of the envelope. Be sure that they will match up when it gets snapped closed!

11. Use pinking shears to trim the angled edges of the flap and the bottom edge. This helps reduce fraying.

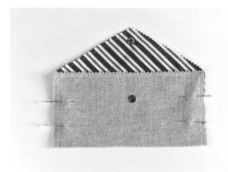

12. Fold the envelope again, and pin the two sides. Sew the two sides, keeping the stitching on the previous stitching line. Be sure to back stitch at the top and bottom.

13. Trim the two sides with pinking shears.

TIP

* Simplify the project by using felt for the envelope instead of linen and fabric. Instead of using a sewing machine, you can even sew by hand!

HEY HEY CROSS-STITCH MAGNETS

Many cross-stitch designs for plastic canvas can look dated, but using brightly colored yarn and modern geometric shapes completely flips the script. These playful designs make terrific magnets for your refrigerator or can be used as a monogrammed gift.

SUPPLIES

Plastic cross-stitch canvas squares	Pencil	Scissors
Graph paper	Darning needle	Hot-glue gun and glue
	Yarn	Magnet

DIRECTIONS

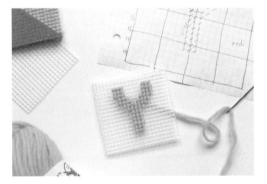

1. On a piece of graph paper, outline a square that is the same number of small squares as your plastic cross-stitch canvas. The ones pictured here are 20 by 20. Use a pencil (and colored markers) to make your design. These tags feature block letters 3 grids wide with a 1-grid shadow.

2. Pick your yarn color, and thread your needle. The basic stitch used on these tags is called a continental or tent stitch—it's a diagonal stitch formed by threading the needle up through one hole and then down through the hole kitty-corner to it. Keep doing this until you're done using that color of yarn, and then tie off on the back.

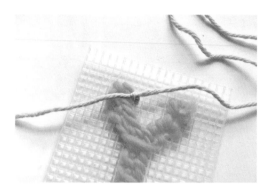

3. Continue in the same way for the shadow—this image shows a close-up of the back of the canvas where the yarn was tied off before beginning.

4. Finally, fill in the background color, again tying off when complete. If the yarn tails bother you, use a small dab of glue to secure them out of the way on the back. Hot glue a magnet onto the back, and let dry.

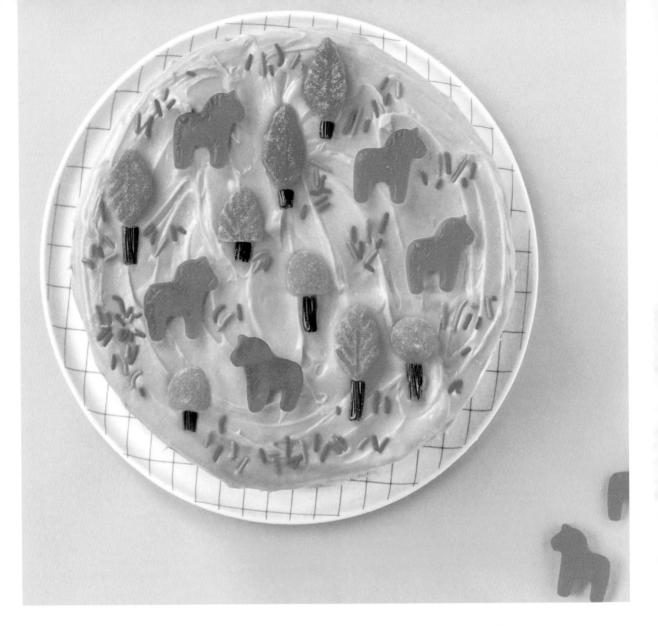

HORSE IN THE FOREST CAKE

Arranging this wild horse candy cake is almost like crafting an ed-ible diorama. These gummy-candy Dala horses are available at most specialty or imported candy stores, but if you can't find them, try shaping and cutting taffy or ribbon candy into horses instead.

Prepared cake, iced with green frosting

Horse-shaped gummy candies

Spearmint leaf gummies

Green gumdrops

Root beer (brown) licorice

Scissors

Green sprinkles

DIRECTIONS

1. Place your gummy horses on the cake. (We used Dala horses from Cost Plus World Market.)

2. For the trees, use a combination of spearmint leaf gummies, green gumdrops, and root beer licorice. Cut the root beer licorice into small pieces for the tree trunks. Place the trees around the cake, mixing and matching leaves and trunks.

3. To finish, add some green sprinkles around the cake to look like grass.

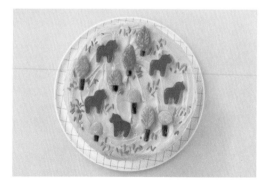

HOT POTATO

Remember the classic hot potato game played at birthday parties? Whoever was holding the potato when the music stopped was out, and the other kids kept playing until one winner was left to receive the prize. This new and improved version uses a papier-mâché potato filled with small prizes instead, so each player leaves the circle with a treat.

Water balloons

Balloon pump

Newspaper strips

Papier-mâché paste (1 cup
flour mixed with 1 cup water)

Multisurface acrylic paint
(white and two shades of tan/
brown)

Foam brushes

Waxed paper

Loofah sponge

Craft knife

Washi tape

DIRECTIONS

1. Use a balloon pump to blow up several water balloons. Tie a knot at the end, and use your hands to shape the balloons like potatoes.

2. Dip a newspaper strip in papier-mâché paste and plaster it onto the balloon. Continue gluing newspaper strips to wrap the balloon completely, doing your best to smooth down each piece. Create several layers of newspaper strips for an extra sturdy potato (to withstand the tossing and grabbing during the game). Allow the newspaper strips to dry. A wire rack is a great option for drying papier-mâché.

3. Once the papier-mâché is dry, use a foam brush to paint it white. Let dry.

4. Use a foam brush to paint the papier-mâché potatoes in one or two shades of tan or brown. Let dry.

5. Squeeze out a puddle of darker tan or brown paint on a piece of waxed paper. Dip the loofah sponge in the paint, and dab off any excess on the waxed paper. Dab the papier-mâché potato with the loofah until it is splotchy all over, appearing to have dirty spots. Let dry.

6. Use a craft knife to cut three sides of a small rectangle on one side of the papier-mâché potato, so you have a small door to fill with prizes. Pull out the popped balloon and shake out any glue flakes that may have fallen inside. Now fill the potato with prizes, and reclose the little door. You may want to place washi tape over the door for game time—the kids can easily peel it back and reseal it during the game.

CHAPTER 9

ICE-CREAM CHARMS

Colorful makeup sponges make the very best scoops of ice cream for these tiny ice-cream charms. Once you have a collection of rainbow-hued sponges, add them to paper cones and top with pom-pom sprinkles. Who knew a backpack could double as an ice-cream parlor?

SUPPLIES

Ice Cream Charm template
(visit hcbook.com/templates)

Colored cardstock

Pencil

Scissors

Colored foam makeup sponges

Multisurface acrylic paint

Paintbrush

Bone folder

Hot-glue gun and glue

Pom-poms

Embroidery needle

Embroidery thread

Safety pins

DIRECTIONS

1. Print out the ice-cream cone template and cut out. Gently curl into a cone, holding its shape, and test that your sponge fits into the top like a scoop of ice cream. If your sponges are too big or small, adjust the template as needed. Then trace the template onto cardstock with a pencil for as many charms as you want to make.

2. Paint a crosshatch pattern onto the wedge to imitate an ice-cream cone. Add other patterns if desired, such as polka dots. Let dry, and then cut out.

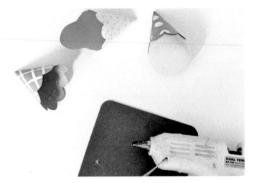

3. Slide the bone folder along the paper while pulling it to gently curve the cone. Roll into a cone shape and hot glue to seal. If your foam sponges vary in size, shape and glue the cone to the exact size needed to fit the foam sponge you've matched to it.

4. Put a couple of dabs of hot glue inside each cone and place foam sponges in the cones.

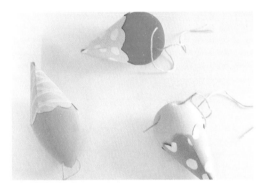

5. Thread the needle with embroidery thread and pierce the foam as shown. Pull the needle all the way through. Leave the thread loose for now.

6. Repeat for all your ice-cream cones.

7. Hot glue mini pom-poms on the ice cream for decoration. Tie the embroidery thread onto the zipper pulls of your child's backpack, or just tie it into a simple loop and use a safety pin to attach it to the backpack.

ICE-CREAM PUPPET

Make ice cream your new best friend with this delightful handmade puppet. Kids will love decorating their puppets with different colored yarn, pom-pom toppings, and cones.

SUPPLIES

2 Styrofoam balls	Hot-glue gun and glue	Tan multisurface acrylic paint
Yarn	Red pom-pom	Paintbrush
Scissors	Red string	Black pipe cleaner
Black felt	Paper plate	

DIRECTIONS

1. Wrap the Styrofoam balls with yarn, using hot glue to secure the loose ends, making sure to cover the Styrofoam completely.

2. Cut out a face from black felt, and glue the pieces onto one of the ice-cream scoops. Glue a red pom-pom on top to be the cherry, and glue a piece of red string to the pom-pom for the cherry stem.

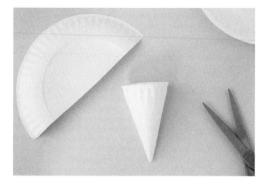

3. Cut a paper plate in half, and roll it into a cone. Make sure the ice-cream scoops fit nicely into the cone, and then hot glue the cone to seal.

4. Give the cone a coat of tan paint, and let dry.

5. Poke a black pipe cleaner all the way through the cone to be the arms; make sure an equal length of the pipe cleaner extends from each side of the cone. Form a loop on each end for hands.

6. Hot glue the two ice-cream scoops together, with the cherry-topped cone on top, and then glue them into the cone.

TIP

* To operate the puppet, simply hold the cone as you normally would and use your thumb and finger to move the arms around.

ICE-POP MONSTERS

Making ice pops is fun any time of the year. Easy to make, the silly faces bring a charming personality to a classic treat. Though they can be made with any kind of ice pop, creamy ones are the easiest and most forgiving. Once made, be sure to let them freeze overnight.

Tray	Smooth-faced ice pops	Edible candy eyes
	(creamy varieties are the	
Waxed paper or	easiest to work with)	Colorful oblong candies
parchment paper		
	Tweezers	

DIRECTIONS

1. Envision, and even draw, the kinds of faces you'd like to create. Consider the placement of all the features.

2. Cover the tray with waxed paper or parchment paper, and set it in the freezer.

3. When you're ready to proceed, unwrap each ice pop and press eyes into place (no need to limit them to two!). Press in other features, such as a nose, mouth, ears, or horns.

4. Set the finished ice pops on the prepared tray, and freeze overnight.

INVISIBLE INK

Channel your inner private investigator or secret spy with this quick homemade invisible ink. Messages and notes will stay completely hidden until heat is applied to the paper. An incandescent lightbulb or warm iron will do the trick.

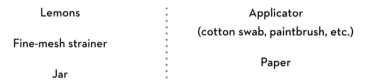

Lemons	Applicator
Fine-mesh strainer	(cotton swab, paintbrush, etc.)
Jar	Paper

DIRECTIONS

1. Squeeze the lemons, and pour the juice through a strainer into a jar.

2. Use your applicator to create an invisible message, a drawing, or a fun pattern on paper. Cotton swabs make nice solid lines, but finer paintbrushes will create more subtle lines. Let dry completely.

TIP

* When revealing the message, parental supervision is recommended. Suggestions for heat sources include an iron, incandescent lightbulb, candle, or electric stove element on low heat. The stove element works very well for larger messages and creates a very even look.

3. To reveal the message, carefully hold the paper over a heat source, and your message will slowly appear.

ICE CREAM

This no-churn recipe is rewarding for young cooks to try on their own, and the simple whipped cream and condensed milk base can be the jumping-off point for a host of creative flavors.

INGREDIENTS

2 cups heavy cream

1 (14-ounce) can sweetened
condensed milk

2 teaspoons pure vanilla extract

16 chocolate sandwich
cookies, crushed

DIRECTIONS

1. In a large bowl using a handheld mixer or a whisk, whip the cream until it holds stiff peaks. Fold in the condensed milk and vanilla. Fold in the crushed cookies (reserving 2 tablespoons for the top of the ice cream).

2. Spoon the mixture into a 2-quart freezer-safe container (such as a metal loaf pan), sprinkle with the reserved 2 tablespoons crushed cookies, and freeze until set, at least 5 hours but preferably overnight.

3. Set the ice cream on the counter to soften for a few minutes before scooping.

CHAPTER 10

JAZZY CASSETTE PEOPLE

Don't throw away those old cassette tapes yet—give them a new life as silly DIY faces! The circular holes already look like a cute set of eyes, so experiment with pom-poms, paper, yarn, and googly eyes to dress them up even more.

SUPPLIES

Cassette tapes	White glue	Scissors
Spray paint	Yarn, pom-poms, etc.	Colored paper
	Googly eyes	

DIRECTIONS

1. Spray-paint the cassettes in an assortment of fun colors. If the cassettes are already colorful, leave them as is.

2. For the mustache man cassette, apply glue to the bottom and add short pieces of yarn. Attach googly eyes over the holes, yarn eyebrows, a pom-pom nose, and a little paper hat.

3. For the love cassette, glue cut-paper hearts over the holes, and draw on eyes and a mouth. Tape a pipe cleaner to the back as arms. Bend the end of each arm into a small round hand.

4. For the cute kid cassette, glue a row of pom-poms along the top as hair. Use googly eyes with a paper circle backing, and draw on a small mouth. Add a pom-pom on each side for ears.

5. For the bunny cassette, cut and glue a piece of pink paper to the middle of the cassette (behind the eyes). Glue a pair of googly eyes on top. Glue two pom-poms together for the mouth. Cut out and glue pink paper ears and white paper teeth. For added detail, cut a pair of slightly larger yellow ears and glue them behind the pink ears.

6. For the bird cassette, cut a triangle of paper for the beak and circles for the eye area, and glue them on. Add googly eyes on top.

JOLLY STORAGE JARS

Channel retro rattan and macramé designs on these pipe cleaner-covered jars. The simple addition of bright colors instantly creates a modern look. Weaving can seem intimidating at first, but the pipe cleaners are very forgiving. You'll get the hang of it in no time.

Pipe cleaners
(assorted colors)

Empty glass jars

Scissors

Multisurface acrylic paint

Paintbrushes

DIRECTIONS

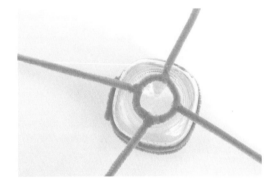

1. Wrap pipe cleaners around the outside of each jar. Depending on the height of the jar, you can adjust the number of rows. Twist the ends together so that they sit snugly in place against the jar, and cut any excess.

2. Form a pipe cleaner into a circle smaller than the bottom of your jar. Twist 4 more pipe cleaners onto this circle, evenly distributing them around the circle.

3. Weave these pipe cleaners up and under the horizontal pipe cleaners to create a sort of grid.

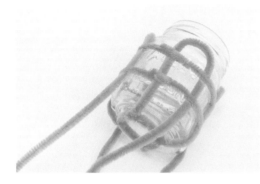 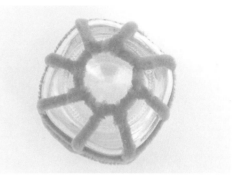

4. If the jar is short, bend the pipe cleaners back and weave them under the horizontal pipe cleaners again, then attach the ends to the circle. For taller jars, though, the 4 vertical pipe cleaners attached to the base may not be long enough to weave all the way back down. If this is the case, twist the ends of these first 4 pipe cleaners around the top horizontal pipe cleaner, trimming away any excess. Add 4 more pipe cleaners onto the circle at the jar's base (place 1 pipe cleaner between each of the 4 already attached so it remains evenly spaced), and weave them up the jar in the same way as before.

5. After the weaving is done, twist all the ends to the bottom circle, and trim the excess.

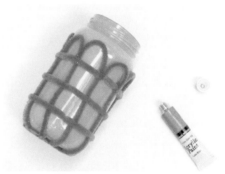

6. Paint the inside of the jar to add more color.

7. Repeat with jars in various shapes and sizes! Mix and match colors, and bend the pipe cleaners to create new designs of your own.

JAM

Take peanut butter and jelly to the next level with homemade freezer jam. This bright, fresh taste pairs perfectly with toast, muffins, or almost any baked good you can think of.

— MAKES ABOUT 4 CUPS —

INGREDIENTS

2 cups crushed raspberries	¾ cup water	½-pint jars
4 cups sugar	1 (1¾-ounces) package fruit pectin	

DIRECTIONS

1. Pour crushed raspberries into a large bowl.

2. Add the sugar 1 cup at a time, mixing well after each addition.

3. In a small saucepan, bring the water to a boil. Add the fruit pectin, and follow the instructions on the package.

4. Add the pectin mixture to the raspberry-sugar mixture, and stir well until most, if not all, of the sugar appears to be dissolved.

5. Pour the jam into ½-pint jars, leaving ½ inch of space at the top. Immediately seal the jars with their lids, and let stand at room temperature for 24 hours.

6. Store in the freezer until ready to use, up to 1 year, or in the fridge for up to 3 weeks.

CHAPTER 11

KEY CHAINS

A trip to the dollar store is all you need to craft these jumbo key chains. Pick out your favorite plastic toys—food, animals, dinosaurs, and, of course, beads—to create key chains you'll never lose. These also make wonderful backpack charms for younger kids who don't have their own house keys yet.

SUPPLIES

Small plastic toys

Multisurface acrylic paint

Paintbrushes

Nail or safety pin

Hot-glue gun and glue
(optional)

Wire

Wire cutters

Scissors

Yarn

Beads (alphabet and assorted)

Pom-poms

Empty metal key ring

DIRECTIONS

1. Start by painting your plastic toys. Give each of the dinosaurs a solid coat of green paint.

2. Use a nail or safety pin to pierce holes into the tops of the toys. (This will only work if the toys are made from thin plastic and hollow. Otherwise, you can try using a drill, or use hot glue to attach the cord later instead.)

3. Cut wire, and bend it to form loops in the tops of the toys. Secure by wrapping the wires together, if you can, to form a strong wire loop or use hot glue.

4. For the strawberries, tie yarn loops through the wire loops on the berries to secure them in place.

5. Decorate the rest of the cord with pompoms and beads. Don't forget to make the loop at the top and attach a metal key ring.

6. For the monogrammed key chain, thread alphabet beads and regular pony beads onto a piece of yarn.

7. Make a tassel out of yarn.

8. Tie the tassel to the end of the key chain, then form a secure loop on the other end. Attach to a key ring.

TIP

* There isn't a right or wrong way to make these—just add toys, beads, pom-poms, and anything else you want so that you have a completely custom key chain!

KISS ART

Create super-quick wall art with a tube of lipstick and a piece of paper. Use a poster board or printer paper and start kissing. Use ruby red lipstick for a classic look or get creative with any shade you like.

| Lipstick | : | Blank paper or |
| | | poster board |

DIRECTIONS

Generously apply lipstick onto your lips, and kiss the page. Repeat this process until the full page is covered. Kiss the page in a grid for a neat look, or kiss randomly all over if you prefer.

KITTEN CLUTCHES

Looking for a simple sewing craft? Our felt kitten clutches are purrrfect! Turn leftover felt scraps, spare buttons, and pom-poms into a fun afternoon activity. Mix and match supplies to make a collection of rainbow cats.

SUPPLIES

Felt (various colors)	Scissors	Buttons
Printable cat template (visit hcbook.com/templates for printable template)	Pins (optional)	Pom-poms
	Sewing needle	White glue
	Thread	Yarn or string

DIRECTIONS

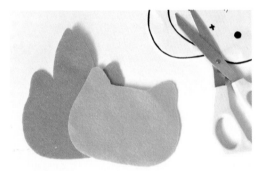

1. Cut a simple cat head shape, about 4 inches wide and 3 inches tall, from one color of felt. Place this felt cat onto a contrasting piece of felt, cutting another matching piece but adding a 2-inch-tall triangle between the ears. If you have access to a printer, visit hcbook.com/templates to print out the exact template.

2. Lay the front on top of the back, and pin together. Use scissors to trim the front ears to expose the edge of the back as shown.

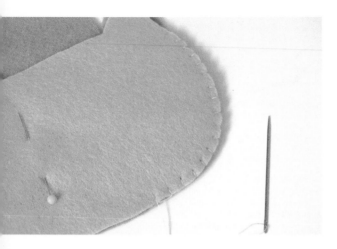

3. Thread the needle, and do a blanket stitch (visit hcbook.com to see a video of this stitch in action) around the edge of the kitten face, stopping and starting before the ears. A simple running stitch can be used instead for younger sewers—just go in from the back, up to the front, then back through to the back, and keep repeating.

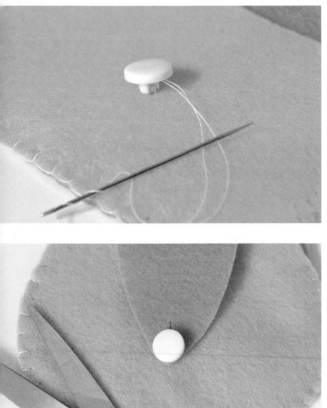

4. Sew the button nose onto the front layer of the kitten's face about 2½ inches from the top, tying a knot to secure on the inside of the clutch. Refer to the printable template for exact placement, if desired.

5. Cut a small snip in the felt flap so that the button fits in as shown.

6. Sew the two button eyes on the front felt just slightly above the button nose, tying the knot inside the clutch. You can use the printable template as a reference for eye placement if needed. Glue small pom-poms onto the buttons.

7. Cut yarn or string into short pieces and glue onto the kitten's cheeks as whiskers.

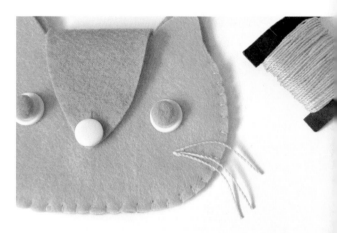

8. Do the same for the kitten's mouth. Let the glue dry completely, and then fill your kitten clutch with treasures!

KOKESHI DOLL STIR STICKS

Stir your Shirley Temples in style with these Japanese kokeshi doll stir sticks. And when the drinks are all gone? Use the dolls to put on a puppet show.

SUPPLIES

Toothpicks	⅜-inch wooden ball knob (⅛-inch hole)	7-inch-long wood dowel (⅛-inch diameter)
Multisurface acrylic paint (black, brown, yellow, pink, white, etc.)	Two ⅜-inch wooden balls	Wood glue
Paintbrushes	1-inch unfinished wooden bead (⅛-inch hole)	

DIRECTIONS

1. Use the end of a toothpick to paint the hair outline on the wooden ball knob. Use a paintbrush to fill in the rest of the hair. Paint the ⅜-inch wooden balls the same color as the hair to use as ponytails, pigtails, or buns. Let dry.

2. Paint the wooden bead in the color of your choice to use as the body. Let dry.

3. Once the wood ball knob is dry, place it on the end of the dowel. Holding it steady, use a toothpick to paint black eyes and a pink mouth. You can use plain circles for eyes, curvy lines with eyelashes, half-circles with lashes, etc. Let dry, and then remove from the dowel.

4. Use a toothpick and white paint to add a pattern to the wooden bead. Paint simple X's, small dots, crosses, V's, or other patterns of your choice. Let dry.

5. Once the outfit is completely dry, slide the wooden bead onto the dowel and push it down until it no longer moves, making sure that the end of the dowel is below or level with the top of the bead. Use wood glue to attach the wooden ball knob "head" to the wooden bead "body." Let dry.

6. One at a time, glue one or both of the painted wooden balls to the top, sides, or back of the head. You may have to lay the doll on its side to allow each ponytail to dry. You will also need to hold the ball in place for 30 seconds to a few minutes until it seems secure enough to hold on its own as the glue dries. Let dry completely.

CHAPTER 12

LANTERNS

These paper lanterns come together quickly. With bright colors and a little paint, they are beautiful to hang all over the house for a party or any day worth celebrating.

SUPPLIES

Colored paper	Scissors	Hole punch
Multisurface acrylic paint	White glue	Yarn
Paintbrush		

DIRECTIONS

 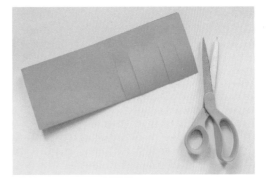

1. Paint a pattern onto a piece of colored paper. Let dry.

2. Fold the paper in half lengthwise, so that the pattern is on the outside. Cut slits about one inch apart along the fold. Leave about one inch uncut along the top edge.

3. Unfold the lantern, and roll the paper into a tube. Use glue to secure in place.

4. Punch two holes directly opposite each other into the top edge.

5. Thread a piece of yarn into each hole and tie a knot to secure. Tie the pieces of yarn together, and hang the lantern.

LEAF PAINTING

On your next family walk around the neighborhood, collect fallen leaves to bring home with you. As you paint them, take the opportunity to talk about and observe their different shapes. Add larger-than-life colors to make them extra festive.

SUPPLIES

Leaves · Paintbrushes

Multisurface acrylic paint ·

DIRECTIONS

1. Before painting, press the leaves. To do this, arrange the leaves in a single layer and set a pile of heavy books on top. It doesn't take long to press them flat, so check on them in a couple of hours. If you skip this step, the leaves tended to curl up and wrinkle, and they may not sit flat on the table.

2. Once the leaves are ready, paint them and let dry.

LEANING TOWERS OF TRAPEZE

Get ready to build the tallest tower you've ever seen! Using plastic cups as the base makes them surprisingly lightweight and ideal for constructing towers of all sizes.

Duct tape (multiple colors)   Plastic cups   Paper plates

DIRECTIONS

1. Select a color of tape, and apply it onto a cup, covering the outside completely without covering the cup opening. Cover a few more cups and paper plates using different colors.
2. Tape the cups together with plates in different formations to create unique shapes.

LOVELY LLAMAS

Create a herd of llamas with one of the most versatile craft supplies—
paper plates. You won't be able to get over how cute and cuddly they
look.

White paper plates : Pencil : Multisurface acrylic paint

Scissors : Hot-glue gun and glue : Paintbrushes

DIRECTIONS

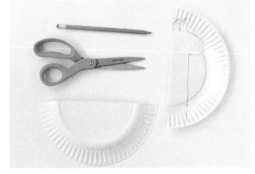

1. Cut a paper plate in half. One half is for the body, and the other half is for the head, legs, and tail. Use a pencil to draw a simple llama neck and head along the cut edge of the paper plate as shown.

2. Cut out the head and cut four legs and a tail from the remaining paper plate scrap. (The legs are simply rectangles with rounded ends and the tail is a small raindrop shape.)

3. Hot glue the head, legs, and tail onto the back of the body.

4. Time for the fun part! Pick out a few shades of acrylic paint, and paint the llama's face and ear details, a blanket for its back, and a collar. Let dry. Repeat to make an entire herd of llamas! Use washi tape to stick them to a wall for decoration or glue an ice-pop stick to the back to use the llama as a puppet.

LOBSTER CUPCAKES

Use gummy candy to make adorable lobster cupcakes. They're perfect for an under-the-sea birthday party or baby shower, or even a pirate- or nature-themed party.

SUPPLIES

Baked cupcakes

Blue frosting

Red licorice bites

Swedish Berries candies

Scissors or knife

Twizzlers Pull 'n' Peel ropes

Big Foot gummy candies

DIRECTIONS

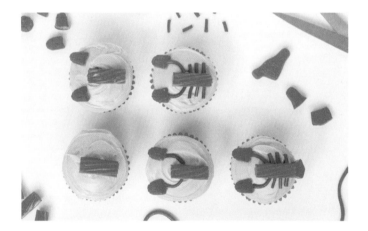

1. Ice the cupcakes with blue frosting.

2. Place a licorice bite in each cupcake's center.

3. Cut a Swedish Berry in half vertically, and place both pieces above the licorice. These will be the claws.

4. Cut 2 small pieces of Pull 'n' Peel to connect the claws to the body.

5. Cut 6 short pieces of Pull 'n' Peel, and arrange them next to the licorice body for legs.

6. For the tail, cut a piece off the Big Foot gummy candy into a trapezoid shape, and place it on the other end of the licorice bite.

LEMON BARS

This classic sweet yet tart treat is a no-fail dessert any time of year. Wrap up a few squares as delicious gifts, or pack them into a container to bring along on your next picnic.

INGREDIENTS

For the crust

1 cup (2 sticks) unsalted butter, at room temperature

½ cup granulated sugar

2 cups flour

⅛ teaspoon kosher salt

For the filling

1½ cups granulated sugar

¼ cup flour

4 large eggs, at room temperature

Zest and juice of 2 lemons

For the topping

¼ cup confectioners' sugar

DIRECTIONS

1. Preheat the oven to 350°F.

2. To make the crust, in a bowl, combine the butter, granulated sugar, flour, and salt.

3. Use your hands to press the dough evenly into a 9 by 13-inch baking pan.

4. Bake for 15 to 20 minutes, until the crust is golden in color.

5. While the crust is cooking, make the filling: In a large bowl, whisk together the granulated sugar and flour.

6. In a medium bowl, whisk together the eggs, lemon zest, and lemon juice.

7. Add the wet ingredients to the dry ingredients, and whisk to combine.

8. Pour the filling over the baked crust, and bake for 20 minutes.

9. Remove from the oven, and let cool in the pan.

10. Dust with confectioners' sugar, and cut into 24 squares. Store in a covered container and keep in the fridge for up to 1 week.

CHAPTER 13

MANDALA COOKIE TINS

Pasta strikes again! Create these mandala-inspired cookie tins using paint and as many varieties of pasta as you can get your hands on. Search online for flower petal mandalas for infinite pattern inspiration.

SUPPLIES

Assorted dry pasta noodles	Multisurface acrylic paint	Hot-glue gun and glue or strong white glue (optional)
Empty cookie tin	Paintbrushes	Mod Podge (optional)

DIRECTIONS

1. Begin by arranging your pasta shells on your cookie tin. Play with the design until you're happy with it. Keep it symmetrical and repetitive like a mandala, or make any design you like, especially if you're making this with little ones. Once you've decided on your pattern, snap a picture for reference later and scoop the pasta to the side so you know how many you need to paint.

2. Arrange the pasta noodles on a piece of scrap paper or covered work surface, and paint them. Let dry completely.

3. While the painted pasta is drying, paint the cookie tin a solid color. If the tin is already a solid color that you like, you can leave it unpainted. If not, give it a couple of quick coats of paint. Let dry.

4. Using your photo as a reference, arrange the painted pasta on the tin in your original design. Use hot glue or strong white glue to attach each of the noodles in place. Let dry completely. If desired, apply a coat of Mod Podge to seal.

MONOGRAMS

Combine Perler beads and stitching in this quick project. Start by creating the Perler bead base shape and then stitch through the holes to create a monogram. When you're finished, glue a pin or magnet to the back to display for all the world to see.

Perler beads

Square Perler bead board

Cross-stitch letter chart template (visit hcbook.com/templates for printable template)

Iron and ironing board

Ironing paper

Embroidery floss

Scissors

Large needle

Pin back

Strong craft glue (suitable for attaching metal to plastic)

DIRECTIONS

1. Lay out a small grid of Perler beads on the board. Use all the same color so it's easier to see the stitched letter when it's finished. For most letters you will need a grid that is 5 by 6 beads. For the letter I, the grid should be 4 by 6 beads, and for the letters M, Q, V, W, X, and Y, the grid should be 6 by 6. You can lay out the beads as you go or refer to the cross-stitch letter chart template available at hcbook.com/templates.

2. Heat the iron, and place ironing paper over the beads. Iron the beads with a gentle circular motion for 4 to 5 seconds. Make sure not to hold the iron in place for too long or the holes will close up. Remove the fused Perler bead grid from the board, flip over the grid, cover with the paper, and iron for 4 to 5 seconds.

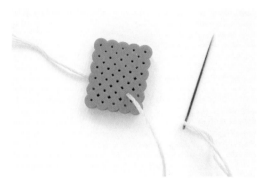

3. Cut a 24-inch piece of embroidery floss, and thread the needle. Bring the floss from the back to the front of the Perler bead grid for the first part of a cross-stitch. Next, take the needle to the back, leaving a small tail.

4. Tie a knot to secure the thread before you continue stitching. Trim the tail.

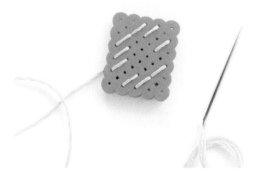

5. Stitch half of all the cross-stitches for your monogram. Try not to jump from one area to another, though sometimes it may be unavoidable. That's okay! If it's easier for you, try stitching a complete cross-stitch for each stitch.

6. Now finish all the cross-stitches. When you're done, tie a knot at the back, knotting the embroidery floss around a previous stitch.

7. Use glue to attach the pin back to the back of the Perler bead grid. Let dry completely before attaching the monogram to anything.

MOON IN YOUR ROOM

Who needs a disco ball when you can have your very own moon in your room? Use a large Styrofoam ball to create a super moon or make a bunch of little ones to hang all over. Either way, your room will be out of this world.

Bottle cap

Pen

Pencil eraser

Styrofoam ball

Foam brush

Multisurface acrylic paint
(white, light gray, medium
gray, and dark gray)

Waxed paper

Loofah sponge

Small foam stencil brushes

DIRECTIONS

1. Use a bottle cap, pen tip, and pencil eraser to poke holes in your Styrofoam ball. Placement should be random, and you may want to make some holes deeper than others to create depth.

2. Using a foam brush, paint the entire ball light gray. Set it on a piece of waxed paper to dry. You may have to touch up the bottom of the ball later.

TIP

* If you want to hang the moon from the ceiling, screw an eye hook into the foam and thread a string through the loop.

3. Use a loofah sponge and small foam stencil brushes to apply splotches of medium gray paint over the light gray base. Allow the paint to dry. Add a few splotches of dark gray paint, and let dry.

4. Once the paint is dry, make color adjustments by going over any areas that appear too light or dark with the appropriate color, and allow to dry.

MOUSE GIFT BOX

Easily make this DIY mouse gift box in a matter of minutes. The next time you have gifts to wrap for a birthday party or special occasion, create an entire family of mice and watch the kids' faces light up!

SUPPLIES

Gray paper

Scissors

Pink paper

Small square box

White or gray wrapping paper

Double-sided tape

Hot-glue gun and glue (optional)

Black marker

DIRECTIONS

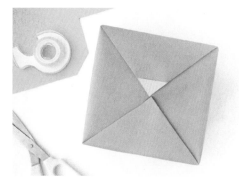

1. Cut 2 teardrop shapes out of gray paper and 2 smaller teardrop shapes out of pink paper. Glue the pink teardrops inside the gray teardrops to make the mouse ears.

2. Wrap the box in gray or white paper. When wrapping each end, be sure to fold the two opposite sides of the excess paper into the box first, forming two folded-over triangles that just touch each other. Cut a small pink triangle, and attach it to the tip of the top folded-over triangle to make the nose.

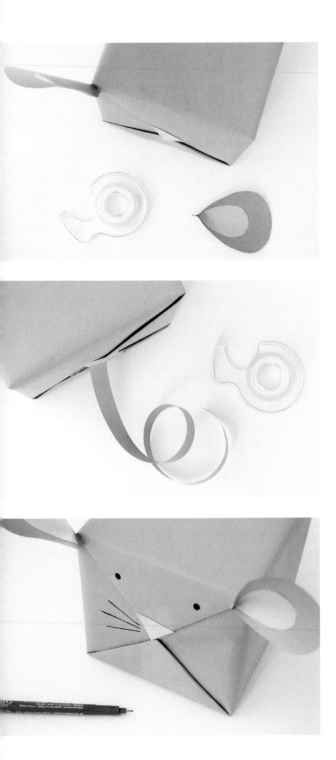

3. Pinch the ears, and attach to the top corners of the box using double-sided tape or hot glue.

4. Cut a 4-inch strip of paper (whichever color you used to wrap the box) and attach it to the back of the box for the tail.

5. Use your black marker to draw two small circles for eyes and three lines on each side of the nose for the whiskers.

MILK SHAKE

Craving apple pie? Get your fix with this simple, creamy milk shake that's absolutely brimming with real apple flavor. It all starts with sliced apples cooked in a light syrup with a hint of cinnamon. Once the apples have cooled, blend them with milk, vanilla ice cream, and a few graham crackers. The results are shockingly apple-y.

INGREDIENTS

For the apples in syrup

1 cup apple slices, peeled (from about 1 apple)

1 tablespoon sugar

1/4 teaspoon cinnamon

1/8 teaspoon allspice

Pinch sea salt

For the milk shakes

1/2 cup milk

5 cups vanilla ice cream

1 cup apples in syrup

2 graham crackers, crumbled, plus 2 pieces for garnish

6 apple slices, for garnish

Whipped cream, for garnish (optional)

DIRECTIONS

1. Make the apples in syrup. Combine the apple slices, sugar, spices, and salt in a medium saucepan, and set over medium heat. Cook for 10 minutes, stirring frequently. Set aside to cool, and then chill in the fridge for 1 hour or more.

2. In a blender, blend the milk and apples in syrup until smooth. Add the ice cream, mixing until just combined. Add the crumbled graham crackers, and pulse once.

3. Pour the milk shake into two cups. Garnish with fresh apple slices, whipped cream (if using), and a shard of graham cracker.

MONKEY BREAD

This monkey bread recipe is sure to be a favorite with friends and family alike. Bring it along to a potluck, or prepare the ingredients ahead of time and pop the pan in the oven while you're finishing up dinner.

INGREDIENTS

3 (12-ounce) tubes
refrigerated
biscuit dough

1 cup granulated sugar

2 teaspoons ground
cinnamon

½ cup margarine

1 cup packed brown sugar

½ cup raisins (optional)

½ cup chopped walnuts
(optional)

DIRECTIONS

1. Preheat the oven to 350°F.

2. Grease a 9-inch Bundt pan.

3. Mix the granulated sugar and cinnamon in a zip-top plastic bag. Unroll the tubes of biscuit dough, and cut each biscuit into 4 pieces. Put 6 to 8 of the biscuit pieces in the cinnamon-sugar mix, seal the bag, and shake to coat. Arrange the pieces in the greased pan. If using raisins and walnuts, put some in among the biscuit pieces as you go along. Continue to coat the biscuit pieces with cinnamon-sugar, and place them in the pan until you've added them all.

4. In a small saucepan, combine the margarine and the brown sugar, and bring to a boil over medium heat, stirring to melt the sugar. Boil for 1 minute. Remove from the heat, and pour over the biscuits.

5. Bake for 35 minutes. Let the monkey bread cool in the pan for 10 minutes, and then invert the bread onto a serving plate and remove the pan. Do not cut! The bread just pulls apart after cooling.

CHAPTER 14

NATURE BINGO

leaf with jagged edges	white flower	red or purple leaves	seeds	squirrel
small reptile	feather	mushroom	pink flower	flowering tree or bush
berries	clover	FREE	body of water	shiny rock
butterfly or moth	litter	ant hill	stick or twig	bird nest
moss	evergreen	thorns	dandelion	long skinny leaf

wild olive for handmadecharlotte.com

NATURE BINGO

clover
seeds
leaf with jagged edges
stick or twig
pink flower

charlotte.com

NATURE BINGO

The next time you go camping, walk in the woods, or even just head out to the backyard, bring these nature bingo cards along. While exploring outdoors, encourage your kids to pay attention to the environment around them, and talk with them about what is safe (and not so safe!) to touch.

SUPPLIES

Scrap paper or cardboard

Scissors

Ruler

Black marker

DIRECTIONS

1. Cut a piece of scrap paper or cardboard into an 8½ by 11-inch rectangle.

2. Use a ruler to draw a 5 by 5 grid.

3. Write a plant, leaf, or any item found in nature into each square.

TIPS

* To play, use stickers, markers, or rocks to mark off items as you seem them.

* If you don't want to create your own custom bingo card to match your location and climate, visit hcbook.com/templates for a printable template.

NIGHT SKY FLASHLIGHT

When the days get shorter and the nights get longer, this project is a fun way to keep little ones occupied after the sun goes down. Shine the flashlight in a dark room and learn all about outer space, constellations, and the night sky.

SUPPLIES

Flashlight	Pencil	Screw punch
Black cardstock	Scissors	

DIRECTIONS

1. Trace the bulb end of the flashlight onto black cardstock and cut out the circle. Then use it as a template to draw more circles onto the cardstock—you'll want a bunch for all the different constellations.

2. Cut out the circles. Make sure the circles fit snugly onto the front of the flashlight.

3. Use a pencil to draw dots onto each circle to make constellations. Punch each pencil mark with a screw punch.

> ### TIPS
>
> * To use, simply place a circle over the front of the flashlight.
>
> * These constellations will display best in a dark room.

NOODLE PARTY

Host a DIY noodle necklace party! The bead prep is easy, so you'll have plenty of time to make a pasta-rific backdrop for your supply table.

Felt	Double-sided tape	Paintbrush
Ruler	Paper rolls (toilet paper roll for canneroni, wrapping paper roll for penne)	Cardstock (various colors)
Scissors		Hot-glue gun and glue
Batting	Multisurface acrylic paint	Glue stick

DIRECTIONS

1. For ravioli: Cut two 8-inch squares of felt with zigzag edges. Cut a 5-inch square of batting, and place it in the center of one piece of felt. Attach long pieces of double-sided tape around the batting, and then place the second piece of felt on top, pressing down to adhere the tape.

2. For penne/canneroni: Use empty toilet paper rolls for canneroni, and cut down wrapping paper rolls for penne. Paint a solid color, adding vertical stripes as ridges. Let dry.

3. For farfalle: Accordion-fold a piece of cardstock (about 12 inches long) and cut triangle snips into the ends as shown. Hot glue the folds together at the center, forming a bow tie.

4. For rotelle: Start by cutting strips of cardstock that are 2 inches wide. Use a strip to form a circle with a diameter of about 1½ inches, glue in place, and trim away extra paper. Then cut a strip into 6 pieces that are 2½ inches long. On each piece, fold a ¼-inch flap on both ends. Glue one flap onto the circle as shown, spacing evenly. These are the spokes. Use another 2-inch strip (you may have to glue two pieces together) to wrap around the spokes. Glue the flaps onto the outer strip as you go, and glue the circle closed, cutting off any excess.

NEAPOLITAN TREATS

Although these Neapolitan treats look just like ice cream, they're actually made using cake mix. Get the best of both worlds—the classic chocolate, vanilla, and strawberry flavors—with no melting mess.

— MAKES 12 CONES —

INGREDIENTS

12 sugar cones

1 box chocolate brownie mix

¼ cup water
(for the chocolate
brownie mix)

1 box strawberry cake mix

1 box vanilla cake mix

6 large eggs
(2 eggs for each mix)

1 cup vegetable oil
(⅓ cup for each mix)

1 cup chocolate melting wafers

Ice-cream sprinkles (optional)

DIRECTIONS

1. With a serrated knife, gently saw off the top 1 inch of your sugar cones.

2. Preheat the oven to 350°F. Line a baking pan with parchment paper (check the box of brownie mix to see what size pan to use).

3. Mix your chocolate brownie batter according to the directions on the box of mix.

4. Cover the top of a 9 by 13-inch pan with three layers of aluminum foil (do not press down the foil into the pan). Make X-shaped slits in the foil, and insert the cut sugar cones in the X's so the foil holds them upright in the pan. Pour some of the brownie batter into the sugar cones (but not all the way to the top!). Bake for 10 to 12 minutes. Remove from the oven, and allow to cool.

5. Meanwhile, pour the remaining chocolate brownie mix into the parchment-lined baking pan. Bake for 30 to 35 minutes. Let cool in the pan.

6. To make the strawberry and vanilla brownies, mix each cake mix with 2 eggs and ⅓ cup vegetable oil. Spread the mixtures into your pans lined with parchment paper, and bake at 350°F for 15 minutes. Let cool.

7. With a melon baller, scoop your chocolate, strawberry, and vanilla brownies into ice cream–shaped balls. Set aside.

8. Put the chocolate melting wafers in a microwave-safe bowl, and melt in the microwave in 30-second intervals, stirring after each, until smooth. Pour the melted chocolate into a piping bag or small squeeze bottle. Put dollops of chocolate on the tops of the baked brownie sugar cones, and attach the chocolate brownie ice-cream balls.

9. Add dollops of melted chocolate between each layer of the vanilla and strawberry brownie ice-cream balls. They might get a little top-heavy at this point, so transfer them to some tall shot glasses or a display that will allow them to stand upright.

10. To decorate the tops, drizzle with some of the melted chocolate, and add a few colorful candy sprinkles, if you wish.

CHAPTER 15

OLIVE STRESS BALLS

Ease your anxiety with a homemade stress ball. This isn't just any stress ball—it's an olive, because "olive being your friend" and "olive you." This DIY is relatively quick, doesn't require many supplies, and will be super cute with all the olive puns available.

SUPPLIES

Spoon

Funnel

Flour

Small plastic water bottle

Balloons
(red and green)

Scissors

Printed notes or a marker

Cardstock

Small hole punch

Baker's twine

DIRECTIONS

1. Use a spoon and funnel to place flour in a small water bottle (make sure the bottle is dry). Fill the bottle a bit more than halfway with flour.

2. Place the end of a red balloon over the mouth of the water bottle and hold it in place. Squeeze the bottle and shake the flour into the balloon. Once the balloon is full of flour, squeeze the neck of the balloon to hold it closed before pulling it off the water bottle. It may have some extra air in it, so slowly let the air out over your kitchen sink, as it may also shoot out some flour. Make sure the opening is facing downward into the sink. Tie off the end of the balloon. If the water bottle is still slightly crushed from squeezing the flour into the balloon, reshape it back to normal and refill with additional flour before filling the next balloon.

3. Cut off the excess neck of the balloon above where you tied it off. Cut off the entire neck of a green balloon, slightly below the neck.

4. Stretch out the green balloon over the flour-filled red balloon. Make sure the tied end of the red balloon goes in first. Shape the balloon a bit with your hands, until it is roughly the oval shape of an olive.

5. Print or write an olive pun on white cardstock, such as "Olive you" or "Olive being your friend." Cut out the words in a strip, and cut a triangle into each end of the strip. Punch a small hole into one end of the strip, and use baker's twine to tie the tag to your olive stress ball.

OLIVE TRADING BEADS

Craft a collection of beads that you can give to and trade among your friends. These oval-shaped beads look just like olives. All you need to do is give them a quick coat of paint and add a red felt pimento inside.

Oval-shaped wooden beads

Green multisurface acrylic
paint (various shades)

Paintbrush

Red felt

Scissors

Rounded-tip darning needle

String

DIRECTIONS

1. Paint the beads in shades of green.
Let dry.

2. Cut pieces of red felt that are slightly
longer than the beads you're working with.

3. Roll the felt and shove one piece
through the hole in each bead, using the
darning needle to help push it along.
Thread the beads onto a string or leave
them as is and trade with your friends.

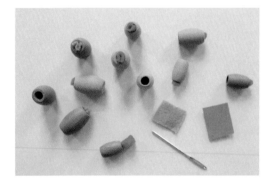

ORNAMENTS

Fill your home with the smell of baked goods as you work with this wonderful cinnamon dough. Although not edible, it has an amazing aroma. Hang the ornaments on a tree, affix them to a backpack, or use them as a handmade air freshener!

1 cup ground cinnamon

½ cup unsweetened
applesauce

½ cup white glue

Plastic zip-top bag

Baking sheet

Parchment paper

Rolling pin

Cookie cutters

Drinking straw

Ribbon

Scissors

DIRECTIONS

1. Mix the cinnamon, applesauce, and white glue together in a bowl. Start by using a spoon, but you can use your hands as well if needed. Transfer to a plastic zip-top bag, and let rest for 1 hour.

2. Preheat the oven to 200°F. Line a baking sheet with parchment paper.

3. Remove the dough from the plastic bag, and roll it out to a thickness of about ¼ inch.

4. Cut out shapes using a cookie cutter, and gently place them on the prepared baking sheet. Poke a hole in the top of each shape with a straw. Bake for 1 hour, and then carefully flip over each shape and bake for 1 hour more.

5. Let cool completely. Tie a ribbon or string through the hole in the top to make a loop for hanging the ornaments.

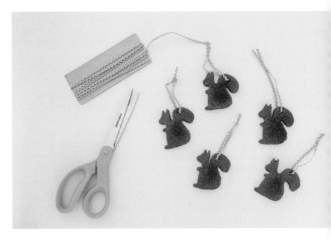

OLIVE OIL CHERRY CAKE

Olive oil gives this cake a wonderful crumb, a perfect complement to the combined flavor of sweet cherries and bittersweet chocolate. This adaptable cake is well suited to many fruits, especially berries of all kinds and stone fruits. Olive oils can vary in flavor, so be sure to select one that has a pleasant, floral taste, as it will affect the flavor of the cake.

— MAKES ONE 9 BY 5-INCH LOAF CAKE (8 TO 12 SERVINGS) —

INGREDIENTS

1¼ cups all-purpose flour

¼ cup whole wheat pastry flour (or use more all-purpose flour)

¾ cup plus 2 tablespoons sugar

¾ teaspoon baking powder

¼ teaspoon baking soda

½ teaspoon sea salt

2 large eggs, lightly beaten

½ cup extra-virgin olive oil

1¼ cups pitted cherries (about 10 ounces whole)

½ cup bittersweet chocolate discs

DIRECTIONS

1. Preheat the oven to 350°F. Liberally butter a 9 by 5-inch loaf pan and set aside.

2. In a large bowl, whisk together the all-purpose and whole wheat flours, ¾ cup of the sugar, the baking powder, baking soda, and sea salt. In a smaller bowl, use a fork to whisk together the eggs and olive oil. Fold 1 cup of the cherries into the wet ingredients. Fold the wet ingredients into the dry ingredients, mixing until just combined. Fold in all but 2 tablespoons of the chocolate discs.

3. Spoon the batter into the prepared loaf pan. Tuck the remaining ¼ cup cherries and 2 tablespoons chocolate discs into the top of the batter in an almost zigzag pattern along the center. Sprinkle the top all over with the remaining 2 tablespoons sugar.

4. Slide the pan into the center of the oven, and bake for 65 to 75 minutes, until a bamboo skewer or cake tester inserted into the center of the cake comes out with just a few crumbs attached. The cake will be a deep golden brown and should be pulling away from the sides of the pan slightly.

5. Let cool in the pan for 20 minutes, and then carefully tip the cake out of the pan. Set upright on a wire rack to cool completely, 40 minutes or longer.

6. Slice and serve. Leftovers will keep well at room temperature wrapped tightly in aluminum foil for 2 days.

CHAPTER 16

PAPER BAG PUPPETS

Turn humble paper lunch bags into playful pets. Make this adorable pair, and you'll have a puppet show ready to perform in no time at all.

SUPPLIES

Paper lunch bags	Paintbrushes	White glue
Multisurface acrylic paint (white, pink, orange, black, and tan)	Scissors	Black string
	Paper fasteners	

DIRECTIONS

1. Give each paper bag a base coat—the puppets pictured use orange for the cat and white for the dog. Let dry.

2. Open up the folded "mouth" area of each puppet and fold the corners of the mouth area under. Paint pink ovals inside, and let dry.

3. Cut 2 inches off the bottom of each paper bag. Use this paper to make the puppets' arms and ears.

4. For the arms, cut 2 rectangles with rounded ends for each puppet and paint to match the body. For the ears, cut 2 triangles for the cat and cut 2 floppy triangles for the dog. Paint pink details onto the ears, and let dry.

5. Attach the arms to each puppet with paper fasteners. Make sure to do this through the top layer of the bag only.

6. Glue the ears onto each puppet. Paint the noses directly onto the bag (or cut out noses from painted scraps of the paper bag and glue them on). Paint the eyes and other face details onto each puppet. For the cat, paint on whiskers or cut small pieces of black string and glue them on next to the nose.

PASTA PLANTS

Make tiny plants and cacti using pasta noodles! Line them up on your windowsill, or turn them into adorable pins or even mini magnets. Take a good look through your cupboard to see what shapes and sizes of pasta you have on hand, and let them inspire your mini plants.

SUPPLIES

Assorted dry pasta noodles (like rigatoni, macaroni, large shells, mini shells, and bucatini)

Hot-glue gun and glue

Thimbles

Multisurface acrylic paint (in shades of green and pink)

Paintbrushes

DIRECTIONS

1. Arrange the pasta into mini plants. For the first cactus, use rigatoni for the body with a macaroni noodle glued to each side. For the second, arrange 3 to 5 thin noodles to look like grass. For the third, glue a trio of mini pasta shells atop a large one. You can also come up with your own unique designs!

2. Glue the plants into the thimbles. Paint the plants green and the flowers pink (or any other color you like), using different shades to add variety to your mini pasta gardens. You can also paint the thimbles if you wish.

PATCHES

Add flair to a favorite jacket or backpack with a custom patch! Create original designs using a few small pieces of felt, a dash of glitter, and a healthy dose of imagination. No sewing required!

SUPPLIES

Felt

Scissors

Glitter paint (in colors to match the felt)

Paintbrush

Stencils and foam brush (optional)

Hot-glue gun and glue (for removable patches)

Fabric glue (for permanent patches)

Pin back (for removable patches)

DIRECTIONS

1. Cut fun shapes out of felt. Use any colors and shapes you like!

2. Apply a matching shade of glitter paint to each felt shape with a paintbrush. If using a stencil, apply glitter paint with a foam brush. Let dry.

3. Trim the felt around the stenciled shapes if necessary.

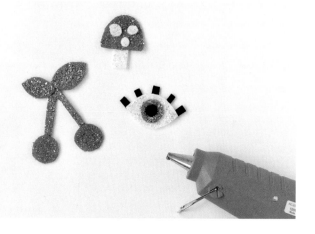

4. To create layered designs, stack various felt shapes and hot glue as needed. Use fabric glue to attach the finished patches to an item of clothing or personal accessory. To make a removable patch, hot glue a pin back to the back side of the patch.

PEANUT PARTY FAVORS

Get ready to go nuts over these adorable peanut piñatas! They're just the favors you need for any party, but especially one with a baseball or circus theme. Fill them up with stickers, baseball cards, bubble gum, or any other small goodie.

SUPPLIES

Balloon pump	Wire rack	Waxed paper
2 water balloons (per piñata)	Foam brush	Loofah sponge
Newspaper	Multisurface acrylic paint (white and two shades of tan/brown)	Craft knife
Scissors		Small treats and prizes
Papier-mâché paste (1 cup flour mixed with 1 cup water)	Paintbrush	Paper shreds (optional)

DIRECTIONS

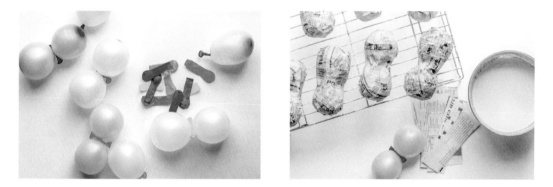

1. Use the balloon pump to inflate 2 water balloons. Tie the balloons together with a double knot at the neck. Make sure to pull them as close together as possible.

2. Cut the newspaper into 1- to 2-inch-wide strips. Dip a strip of newspaper in your papier-mâché paste, making sure it is fully coated, and wipe off the excess by sliding two fingers from the top of the strip to the bottom. Place the strip over your balloon peanut. Repeat this step until the balloon peanut is completely covered. Add a second layer of newspaper strips, plastering them down as much as possible and smoothing out any air pockets or lumps. Once the peanut looks as smooth as possible, set it on a wire rack. Let dry completely (this may take up to 24 hours).

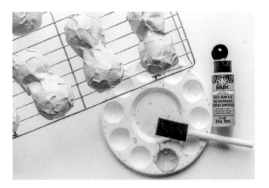

3. Use a foam brush to coat the peanut with white acrylic paint. Let dry.

4. Paint the peanut light brown, and let dry.

5. Use a slightly darker shade of brown to paint vertical lines on one side of the peanut. Leave about ¼ inch between each line, but have the lines meet at the top of each end. Let dry, then repeat on the other side of the peanut and let dry again.

6. Pour a small puddle of light brown paint on a piece of waxed paper. Dab the loofah sponge in the paint and then on the waxed paper to get off the excess paint. (You only need a small amount on the loofah.) Randomly dab the loofah on the peanut, leaving small, splotchy patches of paint. This will help eliminate the gingham look of the lines and look more like "peanut dust."

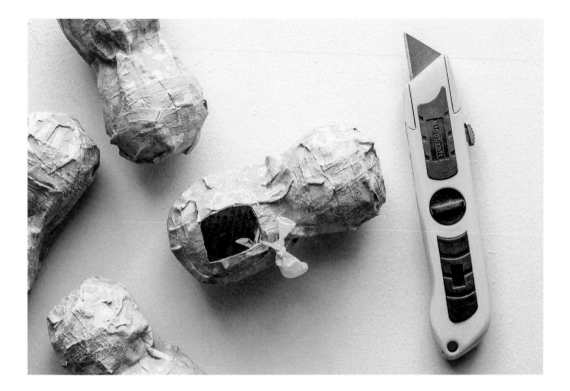

7. Use a craft knife to cut three sides of a rectangle into one side of the peanut, creating a small door. Carefully pop the balloons and pull them out; then fill the peanut with small treats, prizes, and crinkle shreds. Close the door, and secure with tape if needed.

PING-PONG BUNNY CUPCAKE TOPPERS

Turn Ping-Pong balls into adorable bunny cupcake toppers. If you can't get your hands on pink Ping-Pong balls like these, these toppers would be just as cute in white.

Ping-Pong balls	Paintbrush	Hot-glue gun and glue
Black permanent marker	Cardstock	Wooden skewers
Multisurface acrylic paint	Scissors	

DIRECTIONS

1. Draw faces onto the Ping-Pong balls. Keep it simple with black permanent marker, or paint a white oval for the mouth patch, let dry, and then draw the mouth on top.

2. Cut bunny ears out of cardstock, and fold a small flap on the bottom of each one.

3. Hot glue the bunny ears onto the bunny heads.

4. Cut the skewers about 3 inches away from the pointy end. Hot glue the cut, flat end to the bunny's head. Hold in place while the glue dries. The pointy end will go into the cupcake.

PLAY CLAY SWEET SHOP

Your kids will have a blast making their own sweet shop! Play clay is a crowd-pleaser, and with a few kitchen supplies, kids will be entertained for hours.

SUPPLIES AND PROPS FOR PLAY

Toilet paper tube
(or paper towel tube
cut down to 4 inches)

Scissors

Hot-glue gun and glue

Rolling pins

Cookie cutters

Ice-pop sticks

Lollipop sticks
(or wooden skewers with the
pointed tips cut off)

Ice-cream scoop

Play clay in different colors

DIRECTIONS

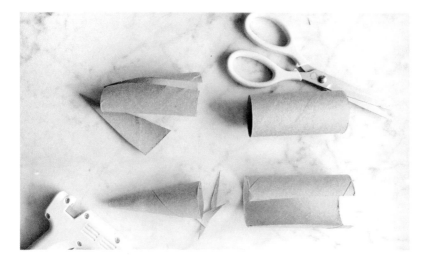

1. For a pointy cone, use scissors to cut open a toilet paper tube down the length of the tube. Cut off a triangle as shown (you can roll it into a cone shape to get an idea of what you'll need to trim off). Roll it back into a cone shape, and, holding the point tightly, squeeze some hot glue under the overlapping seam to secure it. Trim the top to straighten it.

2. For a flat-bottomed cone, use scissors to cut a toilet paper tube down its length. Cut a ¾-inch strip off for the top lip of the cone, and then shorten the remainder of the tube to about 3 inches for the cone base. Squeeze the base so that it tapers and cut off a triangle of cardboard as shown, so there isn't a huge overlap. Taper again, and squeeze some hot glue under the overlapping seam to secure it. Trim the top to straighten. Squeeze a line of glue around the wider top, and place the strip on top of it. Trim the seam as needed.

3. After ice cream and candy-making, the kids will probably want to set up a shop. The recycle bin can offer some more props for displaying their goods. For a lollipop holder, paint a berry basket, flip it upside down, and punch a few holes in it (you can use a skewer). Reuse empty jars to display ice-cream cones.

PRETZEL NECKLACE

Upgrade your candy necklace with this fun twist on this classic party favor! Pretzels are a traditional snack food, and candy necklaces are a loot bag staple, so this project is an adorable "twist" on them both!

DIRECTIONS

1. Cut the string on several candy bracelets, and release the candy pieces into a bowl. Using scissors or a wire cutter, cut a 15-inch piece of wire. String the candy pieces onto the wire, leaving about 1½ inches uncovered on each end.

2. Hold each end of the wire, pressing against the top candy pieces to hold the rest in place. Carefully fold the wire into a pretzel shape.

3. Twist each end of the wire around the wire at the bottom of the pretzel, leaving about 5 pieces of candy between the ends. Wrap the wire tightly and cut off or tightly squeeze the exposed wire at the ends (so the necklace doesn't scratch when worn).

4. Cut a 30-inch-long piece of jersey knit fabric about 1 inch wide. Loop it through the top of the pretzel, going in through the top right side and coming back out the top left side. Bring the two ends of the fabric together and line them up evenly. Tie them into a knot, about 2 inches from the top.

CHAPTER 17

QUEEN OF HEARTS PUPPET

Hear ye, hear ye: The Queen of Hearts is ready to rule her puppet kingdom! She is royally cute and will fit right in with the rest of your puppet kingdom.

SUPPLIES

Scrap corrugated cardboard

Scissors

Multisurface acrylic paint (white and red)

Paintbrush

Pipe cleaners (red and gold)

Gold alphabet stickers

Paper drinking straws

Small round wooden beads

Large round wooden bead

Felt (black and white)

Hot-glue gun and glue

Black permanent marker

Sewing needle

Thread

Wooden dowel

String

DIRECTIONS

1. Cut the corrugated cardboard into a 3 by 4-inch rectangle so that the holes from the corrugation are visible along the 4-inch sides. Paint both sides white. Paint 4 wooden beads and a handful of paper straws white as well. (If you already like the design on your paper straws, no need to paint them.) Let everything dry.

2. Thread a red pipe cleaner through the top channel of the corrugated cardboard to be the arms, doing the same along the bottom for the legs. Decorate the card with red paint and stickers to look like a Queen of Hearts playing card.

3. Cut a paper straw into eight 1½-inch lengths. Thread 2 pieces of the straw onto each arm, placing a wooden bead between them for the elbows. Thread 2 pieces of the straw onto each leg, with a wooden bead between them for the knees. Twist the ends of the pipe cleaners into small loops to be the hands and feet.

4. Cut a hairdo out of black felt, and hot glue it onto the large wooden bead (make sure the hole in the bead is exposed and positioned at the top and bottom of the "head"). Draw a face on the bead with black marker.

5. Bend a gold pipe cleaner into a zigzag crown, and hot glue it to the hair. Cut a piece of straw about 2 inches long, and hot glue into the hole in the bottom of the bead.

6. Cut a piece of white felt about 1 by 6 inches. Thread a needle with white thread.

7. Fold the felt into an accordion and pierce it all the way through with the needle, staying close to one edge. Pull the needle all the way through so that the felt accordion becomes a loose ruffle on the thread.

8. Tie the ruffle around the queen's neck.

9. Hot glue the straw to the back of the card to attach the head.

10. Cut and tie lengths of string onto the head and both arms, and attach them to a wooden dowel. Make a scepter using another sticker and a leftover straw.

QUILT MAGNETS

Want to try your hand at designing quilts? This simple quilt block provides a starting point for a variety of quilts, as you combine and rearrange the squares to make different patterns. Paint with bright colors, add a magnet, and display them on your fridge.

SUPPLIES

Square wooden tiles

Painter's tape

Multisurface acrylic paint

Paintbrush

Gloss sealer

Industrial-strength glue

Magnets

DIRECTIONS

1. Cover half of each wood tile with painter's tape, pressing the tape on diagonally.

2. Paint the exposed side of the tiles with acrylic paint. Paint the edges of the tiles as well, if you like. Make sure to paint lots of pieces in a variety of colors. Try to have at least four of each color.

3. After you paint all the tiles, go back and add more coats of paint until the color appears solid. Three coats should be sufficient. Let dry. Once the paint is totally dry, carefully peel off the tape. If you want to make half-square triangles painted on both sides, tape again and repeat the process.

4. To give the quilt blocks the appearance of being sewn, use a tiny paintbrush or a toothpick to paint a line of white stitches on one side of the diagonal line. Let dry.

5. Brush sealer over the entire top of each tile, as well as on the sides. Let dry, and then add a second coat of sealer. The plain wood will look a little darker when sealed, but it may not be shiny. That's normal. Let dry.

6. Use strong glue to attach a magnet to the back of each painted tile. Let dry completely.

CHAPTER 18

RAINBOW MACARONI

Paint rainbows onto large macaroni noodles to make adorable mini cupcake toppers. It doesn't take long to paint them, glue on tiny cotton clouds, and add a toothpick, so all your cupcakes will be decorated in no time.

SUPPLIES

Multisurface acrylic paint (white and three assorted colors)

Foam brush

Large elbow macaroni noodles

Waxed paper

Tiny paintbrushes

Hot-glue gun and glue

Cotton ball (one is enough to make multiple rainbows)

White glue

DIRECTIONS

1. Use a foam brush to paint the macaroni noodles white on one side. Set aside on waxed paper to dry. Paint the second side white as well, and let dry.

2. Using a very tiny, thin-tipped paintbrush, paint an arch in the color of your choice onto each noodle, following the arch of the noodle from one side to the other. Let dry. Repeat this step in a second and third color, allowing the paint

to dry between colors. Make the final arch at the top extra thick, so that it will serve as the top color on both sides of the noodle. Continue adding colored arches on the macaroni noodles until both sides, the top, and the bottom are all covered in colored arches. Let dry completely.

3. Use a hot-glue gun to place a small bit of glue in one end of the noodle and insert a toothpick, holding the toothpick in place until the glue cools and hardens. Make sure the toothpick will stay in place on its own before letting go.

4. Pull off small pieces of cotton ball, and roll them into clouds. Use white glue to add a teeny-tiny cotton ball cloud to the ends of each rainbow. Let dry.

TIP

* You can also glue the rainbows onto bobby pins or magnets.

RAINBOW PUPPET

Say hello to your new best friend, a DIY paper plate rainbow puppet! Haven't you always wanted a rainbow friend who can dance and do jazz hands?

Paper plate

Scissors

Multisurface acrylic paint
(red, pink, yellow, and black)

Paintbrushes

Tissue paper
(red, pink, and yellow)

Tape

String

2 wooden dowels

DIRECTIONS

1. Cut a paper plate into two pieces, with one piece slightly bigger than the other. Set the small piece aside for another project.

2. Paint rainbow arches onto the larger piece of paper plate, and let dry.

3. Cut long strips of tissue paper, matching the colors of your rainbow and keeping their width about the same as well. Use tape to secure these to the back of the paper plate.

4. Paint a cute face onto the rainbow with black paint.

5. Cut two pieces of string, and attach them to the back of the paper plate, tying the other ends to a wooden dowel. Cut two more pieces of string, and tape one end to the end of the red tissue paper strip. Tie the other two ends to another wooden dowel, so that you can control the rainbow's arms separately from the body.

ROCK PUZZLE

Gather a collection of small rocks, and turn them into a bright and playful puzzle! There are lots of ways it can be arranged, delivering a different flowery result each time.

SUPPLIES

Rocks or pebbles   Multisurface acrylic paint   Paintbrushes

DIRECTIONS

1. While collecting your rocks for this project, arrange them into flowers as you go to make sure you have a good selection of rocks in matching sizes. Oblong rocks can be used as petals on larger flowers, or save them to the side to be the leaves.

2. After all the rocks have been collected, make sure they are clean and dry. Arrange the rocks into flowers in a circle shape. You can use a dinner plate as a guide.

3. Paint the rock flowers in a variety of colors. Let dry completely.

4. Arrange and rearrange the rocks to make different floral wreaths, bouquets, or whatever you like!

ROCKS ON THE BEACH

This playful collection of rock stars was inspired by long days in the sand and sun. Next time you go to the beach, bring these rocks along with you!

Rocks	:	Paintbrushes	:	Mod Podge (optional)
Multisurface acrylic paint	:	Felt	:	Drink umbrellas
	:	Scissors	:	

DIRECTIONS

1. If needed, wash your rocks, and let them dry completely. Start by painting sunglasses onto the rocks—experiment with different shapes of sunglasses! Let dry.

2. Use black paint to fill in the lenses of sunglasses. Let dry. If you want to give your rocks an extra layer of protection and a glossy finish, apply a coat of Mod Podge.

3. Using the largest rock as a guide, cut felt into mini rectangles to look like beach towels. Once you get to the beach, lay out the felt, and put a rock on each one. Pop up the paper umbrellas, and stick them into the sand. Leave as a fun surprise for your kids or friends, but don't forget to clean up everything before you leave the beach.

RASPBERRY-MANGO SMOOTHIES

Sweet and tangy, the bright flavors of mango and raspberry in this smoothie pop just as much as the graduated hues. This striking treat is wonderful for cooling off on summer days or bringing a hint of summer to your day in colder months.

INGREDIENTS

For the mango smoothie	For the raspberry smoothie
1½ to 2 cups orange juice	1½ to 2 cups orange juice
1 cup frozen mango chunks	1 cup raspberries
1 frozen banana	1 frozen banana
1 heaping cup ice	1 heaping cup ice

DIRECTIONS

1. First, make the mango smoothie: Combine 1½ cups of the orange juice, the mango, banana, and ice in a blender, and blend until smooth. If needed, add up to ½ cup more orange juice to help the smoothie blend. Pour the smoothie into a glass and set aside.

2. Next, make the raspberry smoothie: Combine 1½ cups of the orange juice, the raspberries, banana, and ice in the blender, and blend until smooth. If needed, add up to ½ cup more orange juice to help the smoothie blend.

3. In a small bowl, stir together 1 cup of the mango smoothie and ½ cup of the raspberry smoothie to make the ombré midtone.

4. Spoon the mango smoothie into two tall glasses, filling each one-third full. Spoon in the mango-raspberry mixture to fill the glasses two-thirds full, followed by the raspberry smoothie. Serve immediately.

NOTE

* For a less sweet smoothie, use water in place of some or all of the orange juice.

CHAPTER 19

SALAD SPINNER PLATES

Who would have guessed that a salad spinner could be so much fun? Put a small plate into a salad spinner, drip some paint onto it, and get it spinning. For a food-safe version, decorate the backs of the plates, and let dry completely.

SUPPLIES

Tape

Small clear plastic plates

Salad spinner

Multisurface acrylic paint

Mod Podge

Paintbrush

DIRECTIONS

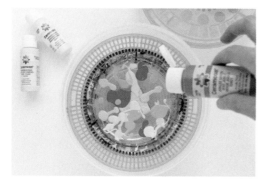 

1. Use a roll of tape to attach a clear plastic plate inside the salad spinner. Make sure to tape it in so that the bottom of the plate is facing up. Squeeze drops, lines, swirls, and blobs of paint onto the plate. Experiment with different techniques.

2. Close the lid of the salad spinner, and spin away! When you remove the lid, the paint will have spread out over the plate. If you're happy with the way it looks at this point, carefully remove the plate from the salad spinner, and set it aside to dry. You can also choose to add more paint after the first spin if you want to add more details and layers. Repeat to paint as many plates as you like.

3. Once you're happy with the plates' designs, let them dry overnight.

4. Give the painted sides of the plates a coat of Mod Podge for extra protection, especially if you plan on reusing these plates multiple times. Use a damp cloth or sponge to wipe clean the top, unpainted side as needed after using.

SAND MILL

Kids who love to tinker and fix things will have a blast building this sand mill beach toy. Gather wooden dowels, ice-pop sticks, plastic utensils, paper plates, and cups. To engineer an even bigger sand toy setup, use longer dowels and more wheels.

Scrap paper

Pencil

Scissors

Paper plates

Screw punch

6 plastic spoons

Plastic drinking straw

Hot-glue gun and glue

Wooden dowels

Flat wooden rectangle

Wooden skewers
and coffee stir sticks

String

Washi tape

Funnel

DIRECTIONS

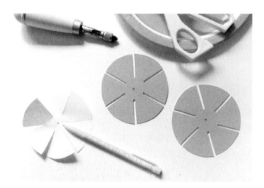

1. On a piece of scrap paper, trace a circle about 4 inches across and mark the center. Fold the paper circle in half, then into thirds, so that when unfolded, there are 6 equal segments. Cut a slit along each fold line, leaving the center ¾ inch untouched. Use this paper circle template to trace and cut 2 identical circles out of paper plates. Use the screw punch to make holes through the center points.

2. Carefully cut the ends of the handles off the plastic spoons, leaving just enough handle that they fit nicely into the slits cut into the circles and the spoon sits right at the edge.

3. Cut a short piece off a plastic straw (¼ to ½ inch) and use a tiny dab of hot glue to attach it around the center hole of one of the plates. Make sure to attach it to the uncolored side. Use another dab of glue on the straw to attach the second circle, lining up the slits.

4. Place the cut plastic spoons into each slit, and use hot glue to secure them in place.

5. Hot glue two wooden dowels onto the wooden base, holding them until the glue cools and hardens and the dowels are secure.

6. Put a wooden skewer through the center hole of the wheel, and then glue the wooden skewer to each wooden dowel so that the wheel can spin without hitting the base.

7. Cut off the excess wooden skewer, and wrap string around the joints to secure, hot gluing the end in place. You can also wrap string around the base of the dowel to hide any visible hot glue.

8. Hot glue a wooden coffee stir stick onto the tops of the 2 wooden dowels, cutting off the excess on the sides. Wrap and glue string around the joints as before, and glue the edge of the funnel onto the very top. Use washi tape to decorate the funnel, if desired.

SEWING CARDS

Kids learning to sew will go crazy for these completely custom sewing cards! Paint nearly any shape or design you can dream up, and easily transform it into a whole set of matching sewing cards. As they say, practice makes perfect!

Recycled cardboard pieces   Paintbrushes

Craft knife   Screw punch

Multisurface acrylic paint

DIRECTIONS

1. Cut the cardboard into postcard-size rectangles. For a white surface, give each rectangle a quick coat of white paint, and let dry.

2. Apply a coat of paint to give a pop of color. On the pictured stitch cards, three colors were alternated between the nine cards for a cohesive look. Let dry.

3. Paint whatever you like onto the cardboard rectangles. The cards pictured are inspired by shapes from nature, including leaves, flowers, snails, and clouds. Regardless of what you choose to paint, keep in mind where you plan to add the stitch details later. Curved details are a little harder to work with, so geometric shapes are a great place to start. Let dry.

4. Use a screw punch to make holes in the cardboard, following the lines of your design. If you don't have a screw punch, you might be able to use a regular hole punch, depending on your design, or a large nail and a hammer (be sure to make the holes on a scrap of wood).

SHIBORI WALL HANGINGS

Explore the Japanese art of shibori with these quick wall hangings! For this project, food dye and paper replace the traditional indigo dye used with silk and cotton, resulting in a process so simple, you'll have a large collection of custom patterns in no time.

SUPPLIES

Food dye	Paper napkins	Tape
Plastic plate or shallow bowl	Wire rack	Wooden dowels
	String	

DIRECTIONS

1. Mix a small puddle of water with a couple of drops of blue food dye on the plastic plate.

2. Fold a paper napkin into segments. Experiment with different folding techniques and number of folds for different looks. Dip the very edges into the blue water, and watch as the color travels up the napkin. Carefully unfold, and let dry on a wire rack or on a plastic-covered surface.

3. Cut and tie string into short loops. Each wall-hanging needs two loops, one taped to each of the top two corners.

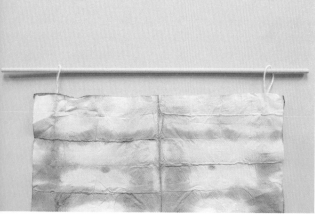

4. Thread the string loops onto a wooden dowel, and your shibori is ready to hang.

TIP

* Thicker, higher-quality napkins will work best for this project, as thinner napkins may soften and tear when they get wet.

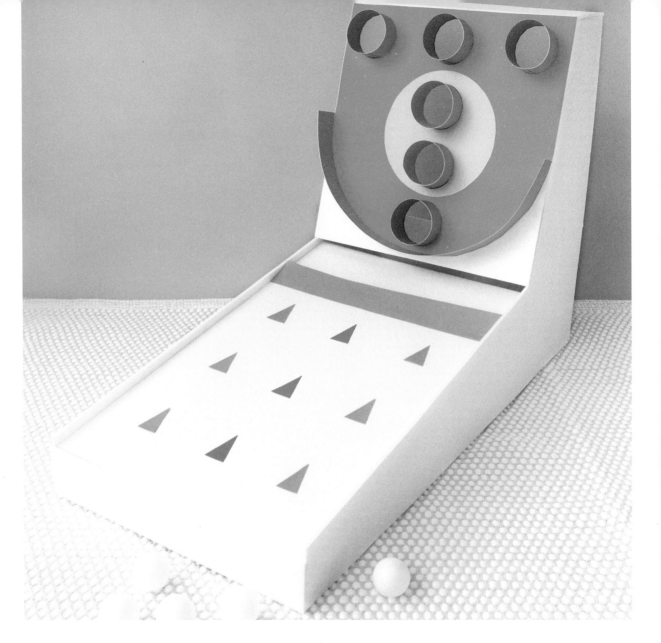

SKEE-BALL

Skip the carnival and make your own games instead! The best part is that you can have as many tries as you want without paying a pretty penny. Assign point values to each hole, and keep track of your score against your family and friends.

4 sheets of foam core	Cutting mat	White glue
Yard stick	Poster board (red and blue)	Hot-glue gun and glue
Pencil	Drinking glass	Packing tape
Craft knife	Scissors	Ping-Pong balls (for gameplay)

DIRECTIONS

1. Measure and cut a 14-inch square out of foam core. Cut a piece of red poster board to cover most of it, but cut a U shape along the bottom edge. (An easy way to get a nice even curve is to tie a piece of string to a pencil to create a giant compass.) Cut a piece of blue poster board into a smaller circle by tracing a plate or another circle from around the house.

2. Trace a drinking glass onto the shapes— one at the bottom of the U shape, two in the blue circle, and another three along the top edge of the red.

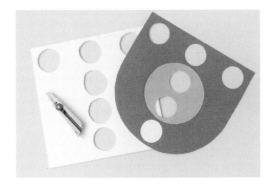

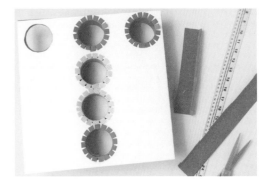

3. Cut the circles out of the poster board using scissors, and glue the red and blue poster board together. Trace the holes onto the foam core square, and cut them out using a craft knife. Don't worry about making these holes on the foam core exact. It's best to make them slightly larger than the traced lines so that the cut edges are hidden behind the poster board.

4. Glue the poster board square onto the foam core square, keeping about ½ inch along the U-shaped edge unglued for now. Cut long strips of poster board that are 2 inches wide and cut flaps along one edge, about ½ inch deep. Fold the flaps up, and roll the flaps to fit into the holes so that the flaps are toward the foam core side. Use scissors and hot glue to secure the flaps in place along the back as shown.

5. To make the side pieces, you'll need two pieces of foam core, one for each side. You can customize this shape however you like or to fit the foam core sheets you have. Make sure that they're both the same shape and that the inner (nearly vertical) edge is 14 inches long to fit the square you already made.

6. Once the two sides are cut, cut a runway piece to connect the two. Make sure that this rectangular piece is the same length as the nearly horizontal edge you just cut on the side, as shown.

7. Begin assembling by applying hot glue along the two long edges of the runway and attaching about 1 inch below the edges of the two side pieces. Do this one at a time, holding until dry. Use packing tape to secure even more on the underneath. Attach the square piece so that the edges are all matched up evenly.

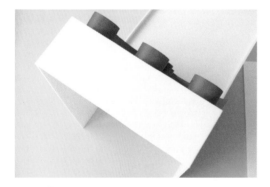

8. Once these pieces are together, measure the very top, and cut a piece of foam core to fit; then hot glue it in place. Do the same for all the other open sides. You can leave the back and/or bottom open if you like, as it won't affect the gameplay.

9. Cut leftover poster board into a rectangle with flaps on the ends to attach into the runway as a slight ramp. Use white glue to secure the ramp so that you can adjust the angle slightly before it's permanently attached. Decorate the runway with arrows or any other shape that you like.

SOLAR SYSTEM NECKLACE

This out-of-this-world jewelry project brings the solar system a little closer to home. Make the planet beads in metallic and bright colors, and in sizes that aren't to scale for a fun and funky look. Kids will enjoy decorating them in imaginative ways.

Round wooden beads
(small, medium, and large)

Wooden skewer

Multisurface acrylic paint

(bright and metallic)

Paintbrush

30-inch necklace chain

DIRECTIONS

1. Select your beads. The largest should be the sun, Jupiter, and Saturn. Use medium beads for Earth, Neptune, and Uranus and small beads for Mercury, Venus, Mars, and Pluto. Arrange them so that they are in order from left to right: sun, Mercury, Venus, Earth, Mars, Jupiter, Saturn, Uranus, Neptune, and Pluto.

2. Paint the sun with a layer of orange and a layer of metallic gold. Let dry.

3. Give Mercury and Pluto a coat of metallic silver paint. Let dry.

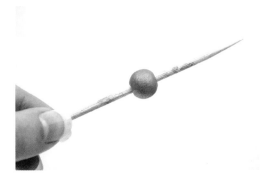

4. Paint Venus orange, with a coat of metallic copper on top. Let dry.

5. Paint Earth blue, and then paint green land areas. Let dry.

6. Paint Mars red. Let dry.

7. Paint Jupiter with metallic copper. Let dry.

8. For Saturn, paint a layer of gold, followed by a layer of silver on top, and finally a ring of gold. Let dry.

9. Paint Uranus blue, with a light coat of silver metallic paint on top. Let dry.

10. Paint Neptune blue, with a stripe of silver around the middle. Let dry.

11. When the beads have all dried, slide them onto the necklace chain in the order they are from the sun.

TIPS

* It helps to place each of the beads on an individual wooden skewer as you paint them.

* For longer-lasting beads, apply a coat of sealant.

* Although Pluto may not be considered a planet anymore, we didn't want to exclude it from the project.

STRIPY STORAGE

Inspired by tropical vibes and bright beach towels, these storage cups add a pop of color and cheer to any workspace. Once you've experimented with the clay, use this technique to make lots of storage in different patterns.

Polymer clay (multiple colors)	Craft knife	Alphabet cookie cutters
Clay rolling pin	Parchment paper	Toothpicks
	Glass cups	

DIRECTIONS

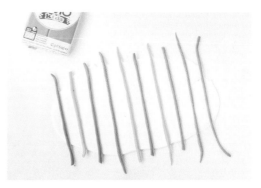

1. Cover your work surface with a piece of parchment paper. Start with one package of white clay for each glass cup (this may vary depending on the size of the cups you're using). With clean hands, knead the clay to soften it, and then roll it out on your work surface. It should be long enough to wrap around the glass completely.

2. Roll out other colors of clay into thin ropes and place them on the white clay to make stripes, like on a beach towel. Use the clay rolling pin to press the colored ropes into the white clay until it's smooth. Play with different shapes and colors until you're happy with your pattern.

3. Wrap the clay around the glass, trimming the top and bottom edges so that it sits flat on the table and so that the top edge is neat. For the seam along the back, carefully press together and cut off any excess.

4. Repeat this technique to cover as many glass cups as you like.

5. Preheat the oven to 230°F. Line a baking sheet with aluminum foil.

6. Place the clay-covered cups on the foil-lined baking sheet, and bake for 30 minutes. Make sure to read and follow all the directions on the polymer clay package.

SWISS CHEESE FORT

Build a play fort out of giant cheese slices. The supplies for this massive play fort are easy to find. When playtime is over, it disassembles easily and can be stored without taking up much space.

SUPPLIES

Yellow foam core	Ruler Pencil	Craft knife Cutting mat

DIRECTIONS

1. Draw a 5-inch slot into the center of the short side of the foam core. Draw two slots along the long sides, about 5 inches in from the end. The slots should be about ¼ inch thick, or however thick your foam core is.

2. Trace circles of various sizes onto the foam core to mimic the look of Swiss cheese.

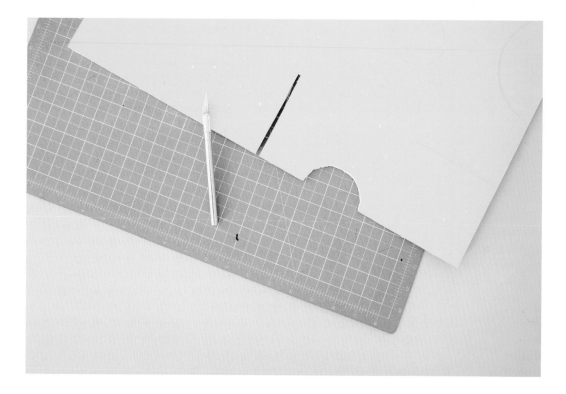

3. Cut out the slots and holes using the craft knife and cutting mat. Repeat this process until you have several pieces of cheese to build a fort with.

TIP

* Experiment with the placement of the slots on the foam core. The pieces don't need to be exact or identical.

SLAB PIE

Large pies are a great way to feed a crowd, and the thinner layer of filling makes them ideal for juicy fruits like strawberries. This strawberry-ginger slab pie has an inventive crust design with polka dots for a cheerful and festive feel.

INGREDIENTS

For the crust

2½ cups all-purpose flour

1 tablespoon sugar

½ teaspoon sea salt

1 cup (2 sticks) unsalted butter, chilled

⅔ cup ice water

For the filling

6 cups fresh quartered strawberries

¾ cup sugar

6 tablespoons arrowroot starch

¼ cup ground instant tapioca (use a coffee grinder to pulverize tapioca pearls)

Zest of 2 lemons

2 tablespoons fresh lemon juice

2 teaspoons grated fresh ginger

½ teaspoon sea salt

1 egg white, lightly beaten

DIRECTIONS

1. To make the crust, in a large bowl, combine the flour, sugar, and sea salt. Grate in the cold sticks of butter. Rub the butter into the flour with your fingertips until well combined. Drizzle ice water over the flour mixture, and gently fold it in, mixing until the dough just holds together. Turn the dough out onto a lightly floured surface, gather it into a rough mound, and divide the dough in two. Shape each half into a small rectangle, wrap tightly with plastic wrap, and chill for 30 minutes or longer.

2. On a lightly floured sheet of parchment paper, roll each rectangle of dough out into a 15 by 11-inch rectangle. Set each dough rectangle on a baking sheet, and chill the dough until you're ready to assemble the pie.

3. Preheat the oven to 425°F. Set a large rimmed baking sheet in the oven to preheat as well (the hot pan helps the bottom crust brown and prevents sogginess). Butter a 9 by 13-inch jelly roll pan or baking sheet with 1-inch sides.

4. To make the filling, in a large bowl, gently fold the strawberries, all but 1 tablespoon of the sugar, the arrowroot starch, ground tapioca, lemon zest, lemon juice, ginger, and sea salt together, and let stand at room temperature for 15 minutes.

5. Working quickly, press one of the sheets of chilled dough into the bottom of the prepared jelly roll pan. Spoon in an even layer of the filling. Set out the remaining sheet of dough, and use a small, round cookie cutter to cut out 18 to 20 (1-inch) circles. Set the dough over the filling. Crimp the edges, brush with the egg white, and sprinkle with the reserved 1 tablespoon sugar.

6. Set the pie on the preheated baking sheet. Bake for 15 minutes, and then reduce the oven temperature to 350°F, rotate the baking sheet, and bake for 50 to 60 minutes longer, until the crust is a rich golden brown and the filling is bubbling vigorously.

7. Let cool for 1 to 2 hours or longer. Slice and serve with a scoop of vanilla ice cream. The piecrust will have the best texture the day it's baked, but the pie will keep, well covered, at room temperature for up to 2 days.

CHAPTER 20

TANGRAM PIÑATA

What's more exciting than leaving a party with pieces of candy from a piñata? How about taking home an actual piece of the piñata with candy inside? All you have to do is make several mini piñatas and arrange them strategically so your design matches your party theme.

SUPPLIES

Tangram pattern	Pencil	Crepe paper streamers
Printer	Cardboard	Fringe scissors (optional)
Copy machine for enlarging	Ruler	Double-sided tape
Scissors	Masking tape	Small favors and candy

DIRECTIONS

1. Do an image search for "tangram patterns" online, and print the pattern of your choice. Be sure to consider how many guests will attend the party and how many pieces are in your design. If necessary, you can make more than one set. Use a copy machine to enlarge the printed tangram to a size large enough to hold candy and small prizes.

2. Cut out each piece of your pattern and trace each shape twice on cardboard. Use a ruler to create a strip of cardboard that is at least ½ inch wide and long enough to wrap around your shape. You may need to tape a couple of strips together.

3. Line up the cardboard strip with a corner of your shape, and tape the two pieces together. At the next corner, bend the strip and continue taping to the second edge. When you reach the final side of your shape, cut the cardboard strip to fit, but do not tape it yet.

4. Cut and tape this final side so that there is a small door for inserting your candy and favors. Do not tape the door closed yet—it should be able to flap open and closed.

5. Flip the shape to the other side, and lay the identical cardboard shape on top. Tape it down in the same way until you reach the little door. Your first piece is complete! Repeat this process to make the remaining shapes in your tangram pattern.

6. Cut a long piece of crepe paper streamer, and fold the piece in half the long way to make it skinny. Use fringe scissors to cut along the unfolded edge of your streamers, leaving the fold intact.

7. Starting at the bottom of your shape, place a piece of double-sided tape all the way across, and place your streamer fringe on the tape. Cut off any excess fringe, leaving a small amount hanging off the side. Continue applying tape and fringe all the way up your shape, layering the pieces and working your way to the top. Once the side is completely covered, trim the fringe along the edge neatly to follow the line of the cardboard.

8. Layer fringe on the sides of your shape again, starting at the bottom and layering to the top. Be sure to cover the door with fringe, without taping down the door. Finally, cover the bottom side with fringe, and repeat for the next shape.

9. Stuff each piñata piece with candy or small favors. Use a piece of double-sided tape to secure the door closed and arrange your pieces to make the tangram of your choice.

TIE-DYE TAPESTRIES

Tie-dyeing may seem intimidating at first, but with some patience and a little bit of practice, you're bound to have great results. If the weather is warm enough, set up your tie-dye station outside to prevent any messy indoor spills.

SUPPLIES

White cotton	Plastic tablecloth	Plastic wrap or plastic bags
Scissors	Wire rack (optional)	Wooden dowel
Tape measure	Tie-dye kit	Hot-glue gun and glue
Washable markers	Gloves	String
Elastic bands or zip ties	Paper towels	

DIRECTIONS

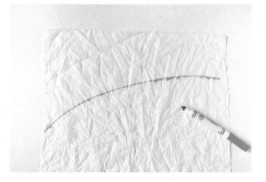

1. Wash your white cotton to remove any sizing. You can also soak the cotton in a soda ash solution (it may come with your tie-dye kit or be sold separately) to enhance the brightness of the colors. Cut the cotton into a square (whatever size you want your wall hanging to be). Tie-dyeing a rainbow is simple: Start with the damp cotton open flat, and draw an arch across it. This will be the top/red area of the rainbow.

2. Accordion fold along this line so that when you look at the folded edge, the marker line looks straight.

3. Use a rubber band or zip tie to bind this marker line. Add more rubber bands or zip ties along the folded cotton to form the other segments in the rainbow.

4. Set up your workspace with a plastic tablecloth covering your table and a wire rack set over it (or directly over the sink) so that your cotton doesn't sit in puddles of dye. Prepare your dyes according to the package instructions, put on your gloves, and have a roll of paper towels ready. Squirt the dye onto each segment, changing colors as desired. Apply the dye on all sides of the cotton (flip it over on the rack as needed). Be careful to keep your hands from rubbing dye around on the cotton by mistake.

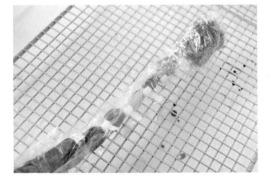

5. When you're done dying, wrap the cotton with plastic wrap or carefully put it in a plastic bag. Let sit for 6 to 8 hours for nice vibrant colors.

6. Carefully remove the plastic wrap or remove the cotton from the plastic bag, cut off the rubber bands or zip ties, and rinse the cotton in the sink until the water runs clear. Wash in the washing machine with hot water and a little bit of detergent, and then put it in the dryer.

7. Trim any of the threads from the edges, and lay the cotton flat on the table. Put the wooden dowel across the top edge and fold the cotton over it, forming a sleeve. Use small dabs of hot glue to secure the edge of the cotton sleeve. Finally, tie a piece of string to each side of the dowel for hanging.

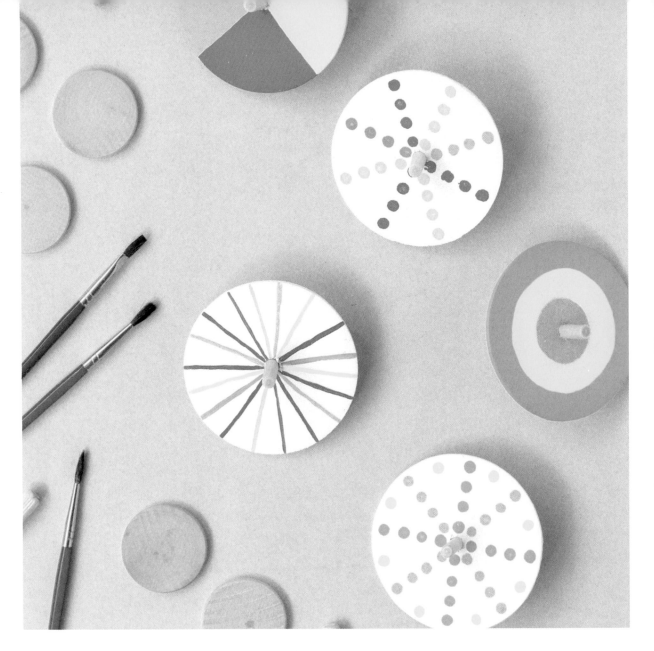

TOPS

Sometimes the simplest crafts are the most fun. These DIY spinning wooden tops are easy to make, and the results are satisfying. Have a blast experimenting with colors and shapes—it's fun to see how different they look once they're spinning.

SUPPLIES

Pencil	Drill and drill bit (matching the diameter of the dowels or pegs)	Paintbrushes
Wooden circles or coasters		Short wooden dowels or pegs
Scrap paper	Multisurface acrylic paint	White glue (optional)

DIRECTIONS

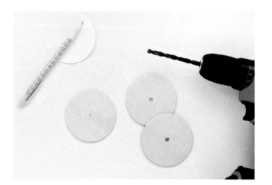

1. Use a pencil to trace a wooden disc onto a scrap of paper. Cut out the circle. Fold the circle into quarters and then unfold it. Poke your pencil through the center point formed by the folds. Use this template to mark the center of each wooden disc. Use a drill to carefully drill a hole through the marked centers. You'll want to make sure that the drill bit you use matches the diameter of your wooden pegs.

2. Paint the tops of the discs. Experiment with different shapes, colors, patterns, and lines. Everything will have a completely different look when you spin it, so it's kind of a fun surprise! Try painting stripes, block shapes, and polka dots as pictured. Let dry completely.

3. Finally, put a wooden dowel or peg into the hole in each disc. It should fit snugly inside, but if it's a bit loose, use glue to secure it in place.

TREE ORNAMENTS

These simple tree ornaments come together quickly with ice-pop sticks and paint. Mix and match different shades and designs so you end up with a whole forest of ornaments. Hang them on your Christmas tree, or attach them to a backpack as a nature-themed charm.

SUPPLIES

Ice-pop sticks or stir sticks	Hot-glue gun and glue	Green multisurface acrylic paint (various shades)
Scissors	String	Paintbrushes

DIRECTIONS

1. Lay out a full-length ice-pop stick to be the trunk of the tree. Cut more ice-pop sticks to look like the branches. Hot glue the branches onto the trunk to form mini evergreen trees!

2. Paint the trees in shades of green, and let dry.

3. Cut a piece of string, and tie it into a loop. Hot glue it to the back of the tree.

TURKEY PARTY FAVORS

Fill these little roasts with prizes and favors to occupy kids during the long wait for dinner. If these little fellows survive Thanksgiving, keep them to reuse next year!

Water balloons (3 per piñata)

Balloon pump

Paper drinking straws
(1 per piñata)

Scissors

Clear tape

Mini Styrofoam eggs
(2 per piñata)

Newspaper or packing paper

Waxed paper

Wire rack (optional)

Papier-mâché paste (1 cup
flour mixed with 1 cup water)

Craft knife

Multisurface acrylic paint
(caramel and white)

Foam brushes

Small paintbrush

Paint palette

DIRECTIONS

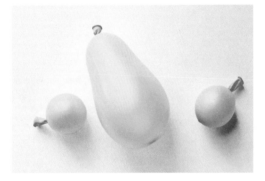

1. Blow up one balloon to full size for the turkey's body. Blow up two more balloons about halfway, and then let out some of the air until you have nice round turkey "legs" that look proportional to the body.

2. Cut your paper straw into four 1-inch pieces, and then line them up side by side and tape them together in pairs.

3. Tape the ends of the "leg" balloons to the straw pairs, and tape the wide end of each mini Styrofoam egg to the opposite end of the straw pairs.

4. Finally, fold a piece of tape into a circle and tape the legs to the body, slightly underneath it and with the balloon end of the legs at the wider end of the body. Tape the end of the "body" balloon against the balloon.

5. Cut the newspaper into 1- to 2-inch-wide strips. Line your work surface with waxed paper, and set a wire rack on the waxed paper. Coat a newspaper strip in the papier-mâché paste, wiping off any excess by running your fingers down the strip from top to bottom, and smooth it out over the balloon "roast." Continue to stick the newspaper strips to the roast until

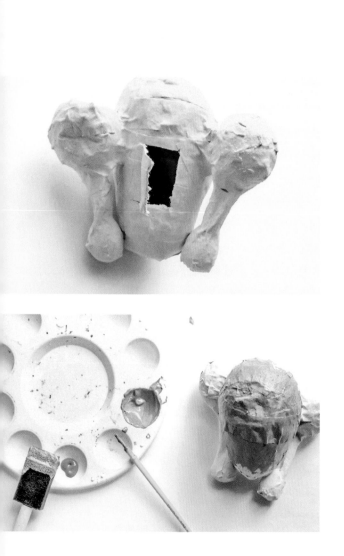

it is completely covered. Set the "roast" on the rack, and let dry overnight; then apply a second coat of newspaper strips, and set on wire rack to dry overnight, or until newspaper has hardened and feels completely dry to the touch.

6. Once the second coat of papier-mâché is dry, use a craft knife to cut three sides of a rectangle on the bottom of the turkey to make a door for filling with candy or prizes. Carefully pop the balloon that makes up the turkey's body. You will need to be able to stick two fingers in to pull the balloon out of the turkey body. It should come out easily.

7. Paint the turkey body a caramel color using your foam brush. Mix a little bit of caramel paint with white, and use this mix to paint the bone at the end of each leg. Allow the paint to dry, and then fill your piñata with paper shreds or confetti and goodies! Close the door, and seal with tape if necessary.

CHAPTER 21

UNDER THE SEA MACARONI WREATH

Have you embraced pasta as a craft supply yet? The fun and unique shapes can be combined in so many ways, providing a variety of different looks and textures. With a coat of paint, this wreath made of orecchiette pasta takes on the look of miniature seashells. Adorn with additional pasta shapes for the ultimate under-the-sea look.

SUPPLIES

Styrofoam wreath form (9 to 10-inch)

Hot-glue gun and glue

Variety of pasta noodles (like orecchiette, macaroni, campanelle, fiorelli, small shells, and large shells)

Multisurface acrylic paint

Paintbrush

Plastic shell toy (optional)

DIRECTIONS

1. To make the base layer of shells covering the wreath form, hot glue orecchiette pasta into three rows, offsetting the shells in each row as you go. Leave the back of the wreath form plain, attaching the orecchiette to the front and sides only, so that the wreath sits nicely on your work surface.

2. Add a row of small shells after the three rows of orecchiette, and then glue three more rows of orecchiette, repeating the pattern.

3. Continue gluing orecchiette and small shells in this same way until the entire wreath is covered.

4. Paint your pasta-covered wreath using multisurface acrylic paint, and let dry. It may take a few coats to get every side of the pasta.

5. Use a slightly lighter or darker shade of paint to add line details onto the orecchiette to make them look like baby clam shells.

6. Paint additional pasta noodles, and a plastic shell if you like, to add on top of the wreath.

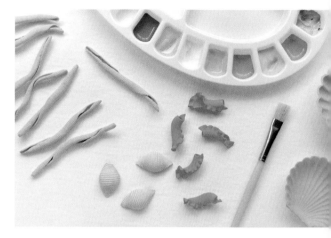

7. Once all the paint is dry, use a hot-glue gun to secure the pasta accents on top of the wreath. It can help to set up your arrangement to the side first, so that you're happy with the design and shape.

TIP

* Hang your wreath on a nail or hook directly from the wreath form, or hot glue a ribbon loop onto the back if needed.

UNEXPECTED ENCOURAGEMENT

Who doesn't love a surprise? Decorate the bottoms of paper plates and cups before your next party or picnic. When your guests finish eating, have them flip over the plates and cups for some positive encouragement.

SUPPLIES

Paper cups		Ink pad
Alphabet stamps		Paper plates

DIRECTIONS

1. Flip over your paper cups and stamp a short, happy message onto the bottom.

2. Do the same for the paper plates. Here you can write a longer message with the stamps.

TIP

* You can also use markers, crayons, paint, and stickers to write these positive messages if you don't have stamps available.

JOB

KNEW YOU
OULD DO IT!
AWESOME'
JOB!

HIP
HIP
HOORAY!

YOU ARE
SERIOUSLY
THE COOLEST
PERSON
I KNOW

UNICORN PUPPET

Craft a playful rainbow unicorn puppet from basic supplies. Pipe cleaners make an excellent mane and tail, while painted pasta noodles and a recycled paper roll form the legs and body. Mix and match paint and pipe cleaner colors to create puppets in every color of the rainbow.

SUPPLIES

Rigatoni pasta noodles

8 small round wooden beads

1 large round wooden bead

1 spool-shaped wooden bead

Multisurface acrylic paint
(white)

Paintbrush

Toilet paper tube

Pipe cleaners (white, pink,
yellow, green, and blue)

Scissors

White cardstock

Hot-glue gun and glue

Black permanent marker

String

Wooden dowel

DIRECTIONS

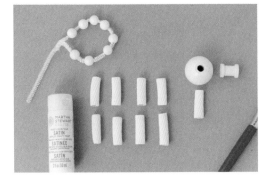

1. Paint 9 pasta noodles and all the wooden beads with white paint. Let dry.

2. Cut the toilet paper tube open along its length and paint white as well.

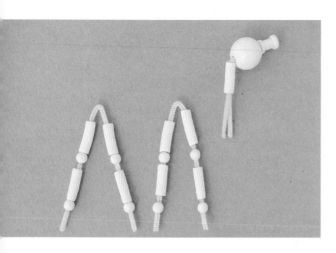

3. Bend 3 white pipe cleaners in half. To make the two sets of legs, thread the noodles and beads onto each as shown. With the third pipe cleaner, thread the spool bead along to the end of the fold, followed by the large wooden bead and the final noodle.

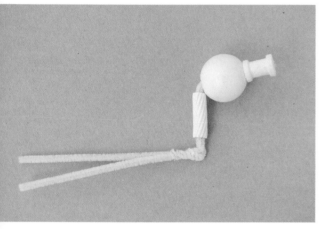

4. Connect the neck pipe cleaner to another folded pipe cleaner.

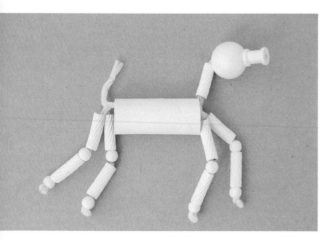

5. Twist the two sets of legs onto the body pipe cleaner, leaving the excess at the end for the tail later. Trim and roll the flat paper roll tube into a new, narrower tube, and set on the pipe cleaner body. Form feet at the bottom of each pipe cleaner by making a small loop.

6. Cut 2 small ears out of white cardstock.

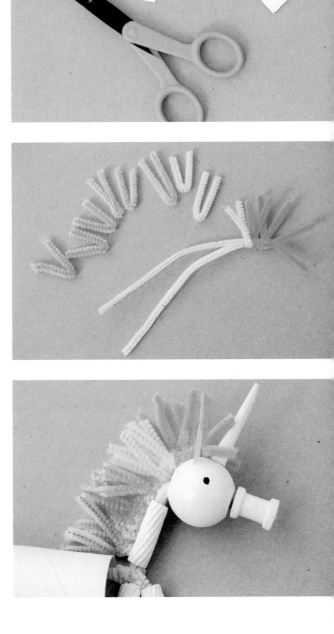

7. Bend a white pipe cleaner in half. Cut 3-inch lengths of pink, yellow, green, and blue pipe cleaners, and fold them each in half. Twist them onto the white pipe cleaner to be the mane.

8. Hot glue the mane onto the unicorn's head and neck, along with the two ears. Use a black marker to draw on the eyes, and roll a mini horn out of white cardstock, hot gluing in place.

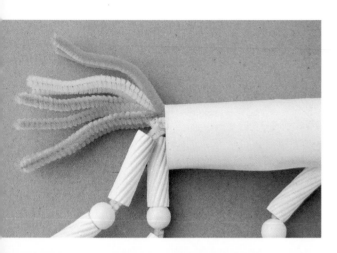

9. Make a matching tail with more colorful pipe cleaners, twisting the excess white body pipe cleaner around them, and then trimming any excess.

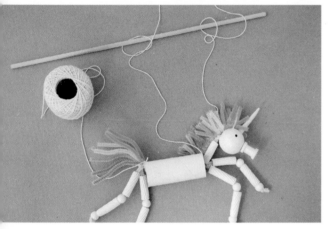

10. Cut and tie white string onto the unicorn's head, neck, and base of her tail, tying the other ends of the strings to a wooden dowel.

URCHIN ICE CREAM

The next time you're visiting a beach town, be sure to buy some sea
urchins to craft with! They make perfect double-scooped ice-cream
cones, a great souvenir that you can make yourself.

Hot-glue gun and glue	2 sea urchin shells	String
	1 cone-shaped shell	1 red pom-pom

DIRECTIONS

1. Hot glue the two sea urchins together to form a double-scooped ice cream.

2. Glue the cone-shaped shell to the bottom sea urchin.

3. Tie a string loop, and hot glue the end into the top of the sea urchin. Top it all off with a mini pom-pom cherry.

UPSIDE-DOWN PINEAPPLE CAKE

Turn a frown upside-down with this classic dessert. The simple recipe is perfect to make with kids, and the final reveal at the end is an exciting one to watch.

INGREDIENTS

For the topping

4 tablespoons (½ stick) unsalted butter, melted

⅔ cup packed brown sugar

10 pineapple rings, patted dry

Maraschino cherries

For the cake

½ cup (1 stick) unsalted butter, at room temperature

½ cup packed brown sugar

¼ cup granulated sugar

2 large eggs, at room temperature

1 tablespoon pure vanilla extract

1½ cups flour

1½ teaspoons baking powder

½ teaspoon salt

½ cup milk, at room temperature

DIRECTIONS

1. Preheat the oven to 350°F.

2. To make the topping, pour the melted butter into a 9-inch round pan and spread it all around. Sprinkle the brown sugar on top.

3. Arrange the pineapple rings in the pan, cutting them to fit along the edges if necessary. Place a cherry into the center of each pineapple ring. Set the pan aside.

4. To make the cake, in a medium bowl blend the butter, brown sugar, and granulated sugar with a hand mixer until creamy

5. One at a time, add the eggs, mixing well after each one. Mix in the milk and vanilla.

6. In another medium bowl, combine the flour, baking powder, and salt.

7. Slowly mix the dry ingredients into the wet ingredients until combined. Do not overmix.

8. Pour the batter into the pan on top of the pineapple.

9. Bake for about 45 minutes, until a toothpick inserted into the center of the cake comes out clean.

10. Let cool in the pan for at least 15 minutes. Place a plate over the top of the pan. Wearing oven mitts, hold the plate and pan together, and flip. Remove the pan. The cake should release from the pan onto the plate.

CHAPTER 22

VALENTINE'S DAY WREATH

This DIY wreath is the perfect way to add some love to your front door or anywhere in your home. Use pipe cleaners to add simple sculptural details. Combine pink, red, and white for a classic Valentine's Day feel, or use other colors for virtually endless combinations.

SUPPLIES

Foam wreath

Multisurface acrylic paint

Paintbrush

Scissors

Pipe cleaners

Washi tape

Hot-glue gun and glue

DIRECTIONS

1. Paint the foam wreath pink, and let dry completely.

2. To make the X's, cut a piece of pipe cleaner about 2¼ inches long each. For the O's, cut a pipe cleaner in half and wrap around a roll of washi tape. Twist the ends together.

3. Stick the pointed twists of the O's into the edge of the painted wreath, and then form the X's with two of the pipe cleaners you cut.

4. Repeat all the way around the wreath.

5. To decorate the rest of the wreath, bend pipe cleaners into zigzags and hot glue onto the wreath.

6. Repeat with other colors until covered.

VEGGIE BLOCKS

Look no further than your refrigerator to create this super-fun, all-in-one snack and game. Grab your carrots and radishes, and see how high you can go!

Carrots	Celery	Cutting board
White radishes	Paring knife	Waxed paper (for playing surface)

DIRECTIONS

1. Cut the vegetables into pieces about 3 inches long.

2. To make the carrot and radish blocks, level off each carrot and radish piece on four sides and then cut the pieces to approximately the same size, keeping them as even as possible.

3. For the celery blocks, trim the pieces, again, keeping them as even and rectangular as possible.

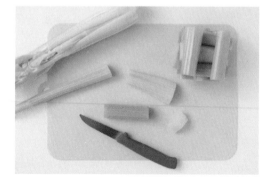

VEGGIE KNOTS

If you have a pile of old T-shirts that don't fit anymore, don't toss them into the rag bin just yet! With just a few scraps of fabric and a pair of scissors, you can turn them into a play garden filled with veggies.

Fabric noodles (fabric cut into 1-inch-wide strips) in assorted colors

Scissors

DIRECTIONS

1. To make a radish, take 3 red noodles and fold them each at the center. Tie the folded ends together into an overhand knot.

2. Divide the 6 strands into 3 pairs and braid them together. Tie a knot at the end, and leave a few strands remaining for a more tapered look, if you wish.

3. Take another red noodle, and wrap it around the braid. When it's all wrapped, do the same with another noodle, building the shape of the radish.

4. When you're happy with the shape, wrap any loose ends under the rest. No glue is needed, but you may choose to use some if you'd like them to be extra secure.

5. To make the stems, tie a few green noodles to the loop at the top.

6. Use scissors to snip and trim the green noodles into leaves.

TIPS

* Repeat the same process using different colors to make a variety of root vegetables.

* Making these vegetables is not an exact art. Experiment with different colors and braiding techniques. You can always unwrap them if you want to make a change!

VICTORY LAP VILLAGE

Zoom around a miniature village made of recycled boxes! Be sure to cut lots of tunnels so that you can make a few extra victory laps.

Scrap corrugated cardboard	Pencil	Craft knife
White glue	Ruler	Multisurface acrylic paint
	Empty cardboard boxes	Paintbrushes

DIRECTIONS

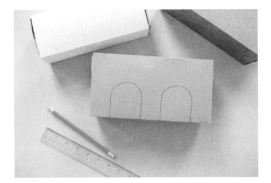

1. Use a pencil and ruler to draw arches on the cardboard boxes. Do this on the front and back sides so that they match up, forming a tunnel.

2. Cut out carefully, using a craft knife.

3. Paint windows and stripes to decorate the village.

CHAPTER 23

WALNUT LLAMA ORNAMENTS

Deck the halls with lots of llamas! Craft a whole herd using walnuts, pasta, paint, and wool roving. If you don't have any wool roving on hand, yarn or cotton balls can be used instead.

SUPPLIES

Multisurface acrylic paint (pink)	Walnuts (in shells)	Black permanent marker
Paintbrush	White glue	Pink wool roving
	Mini pasta shells	String

DIRECTIONS

1. Paint a walnut pink. Let dry.

2. Glue two mini pasta shells on top to be the ears, and give them a coat of pink paint. Let dry.

3. Use a black marker to draw the llama's face.

4. Take a small tuft of wool roving, and shape into a small pile; then glue to the top of the llama's head. Make a loop of string, and glue it on top.

WALRUS COSTUME

Need a last-minute costume? This playful walrus can be created from materials you probably already have at home or can find on a quick trip to the dollar store.

SUPPLIES

3 paper plates

Glue

Multisurface acrylic paint (gray)

Paintbrush

Paper (pink, blue, black, and white)

Scissors

Black and white cardstock

String

Tape

Striped shirt

Gray pants

Gray flippers (optional)

DIRECTIONS

1. Glue the plates together as pictured, and paint gray. Let dry.

2. Cut out a star using blue paper and a heart using pink paper. Glue to the plates.

3. Use scissors to cut out the eyes. Don't forget to measure first to make sure the eyes are in the right location for the person wearing the mask.

4. Glue on a small triangle nose cut from black cardstock, and glue three small black circles onto each cheek. Cut two long tusks from white cardstock, and glue them to the back of the plates.

TIP

* Pair with a striped shirt, gray pants, and gray flippers to complete the costume.

5. Tape a piece of string to the back of each side of the mask. Tie into a bow to secure onto the wearer's head.

WATERCOLOR WINDSOCKS

These windsocks will blow you away! Inspired by Japanese carp windsocks, also known as koinobori, these paper versions are simple to assemble, so you can focus on coming up with fun designs.

White paper	Watercolor resist	Cotton swabs
Printable fish template (visit hcbook.com/templates for printable template)	Paintbrushes	Scissors
	Watercolor paints	Double-stick tape
Pencil	Small dishes or containers	String

DIRECTIONS

1. Fold a piece of white paper in half lengthwise, and draw a simple, long fish outline so that the fold remains as is. Add outlines of eyes, fins, gills, etc., and unfold the paper, transferring all lines to the other half, creating a mirror image. You can also visit hcbook.com/templates to access a ready-to-use template if you wish. Lay another piece of white copy paper on top of your template so that you see the outlines through it. With a small brush, apply watercolor resist over the areas you'd like to remain white. Use your template as a guide, and have fun with it—add scales, stripes, polka dots, or change the fins. When done, let the resist dry completely.

2. If using tubes of watercolor paints, squeeze a little bit of paint into each container and add water, stirring to mix. If using watercolors in a tray, add water and mix in place. Add as little or as much water as you like for different looks, and test them out on a scrap of paper.

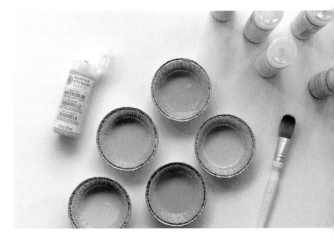

3. Apply the watercolor over the resist-painted fish. For a cleaner look, use a cotton swab to wipe away excess paint that sits on top of the resist. Most of it should bead right off, but the cotton swab helps tidy even more.

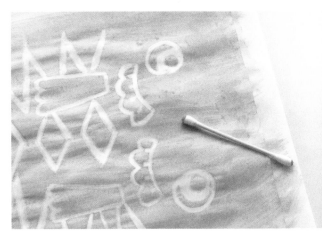

4. Use another color to add details to the fish. When done, allow to dry completely.

5. Gently fold the paper in half without creasing the center. Cut along the edge of the fish, referring to the template. Use double-stick tape to secure the top edge of the fish, forming a paper tube.

6. Cut a piece of string, and tape it into the open mouth of the fish. Hang the windsock fish on a hook or dowel near a breezy window, and enjoy the show!

WATERMELON CHARMS

Summer never has to end as long as you have these playful watermelon charm necklaces. Use a single one as a pendant, or if you want to make a real fashion statement, wear them all at once.

Styrofoam balls

Craft knife

Instant papier-mâché mix
(or mix your own)

Multisurface acrylic paint
(in shades of red and green)

Paintbrushes

Black permanent marker

Wire

Wire cutters

Glue (optional)

String

DIRECTIONS

1. Use a craft knife to carefully cut the Styrofoam balls into 6 wedges each.

2. Add water to the instant papier-mâché pulp, and mix. Apply to the Styrofoam wedges, rubbing to smooth and keep them even. Let dry completely.

3. Paint the wedges to look like watermelon slices. Let dry.

4. Use a black marker to draw seeds onto the watermelon slices.

5. Cut a piece of wire about 2 inches long and bend into a "U" shape. Insert into the watermelon slice to create a charm. Apply glue around the wire to make the joint more secure if needed.

6. Thread the watermelons onto a string to make a necklace, or tie a loop around each one individually to use as charms.

WISH UPON A WREATH CAKE

Transform a store-bought cake into something spectacular. This gummy floral wreath can be made in minutes with just a few bags of candy. Pastel gummies of various shapes and sizes become beautiful flowers, with a variety of green candy leaves and licorice serving as the stems.

SUPPLIES

Frosted round cake

Assorted candy
(gum balls, etc.)

Jellybeans

Gum drops

Floral gummy candy

Spearmint leaves

Green sour rope

Scissors

DIRECTIONS

1. Arrange about three larger flowers first, using individual candies as the centers and petals.

2. Add in smaller gummy flowers in small groupings.

3. Fill in the gaps with spearmint leaves.

4. Cut sour candy ropes into short pieces and add nearby the leaves.

CHAPTER 24

XYLOPHONE

Glass vases and food dye from the dollar store are transformed into a spectacular music-making experience. Have fun experimenting on your own or with a friend, creating harmonies and writing your own songs and jingles.

SUPPLIES

Masking tape

Black permanent marker

27 identical large glass cylindrical flower vases

2 packages of food dye (primary colors)

Funnel (optional)

Turkey baster

Wooden skewers

White glue

Gum balls

Rubbing alcohol

DIRECTIONS

1. Assign and label each vase with the numbers 1 to 26.

2. Stick a stripe of masking tape lengthwise from top to bottom on the extra vase.

3. Measure the height of your vase. Divide the height measurement by 26 and mark 26 equally spaced tick marks onto the tape on the extra vase.

4. Using the extra vase as your guide, transfer the first tick mark onto vase 1 with a permanent marker. Do the same with the second tick mark on vase 2. Continue this process until all 26 vases are marked.

5. Arrange them on your work surface, in order, so that vase 1 is the fullest and vase 26 is nearly empty. Fill the extra vase with water all the way up to the top line. Add red food dye until you're happy with the color, and then pour into vase 1.

6. Do the same for orange: Fill the extra vase to the top, add red and yellow food dye to make orange, and then pour into vase 5. Repeat this for yellow (pour into 9), green (pour into 13), blue (pour into 17), indigo (pour into 21), and violet (pour into 24).

7. All seven colors should now be in their vases and filled up only to the tick marks.

8. The glasses in between each of the colors need to gradually change shades. Mix these colors in the extra vase again, and pour up to the tick marks in the corresponding vases. This step will take a little bit of experimentation as well as trial and error. Use the turkey baster to make slight adjustments as needed.

9. Once all vases are filled and the rainbow is complete, make mallets by piercing a wooden skewer into a gum ball. Use glue to secure in place if needed.

10. Apply rubbing alcohol onto a paper towel, and rub to remove the permanent marker lines on the vases.

TIP

* Experiment with playing tunes on the xylophone. Harmonize with friends, and experiment with the sounds to create songs. If you assign a letter of the alphabet to each vase, what does your name sound like?

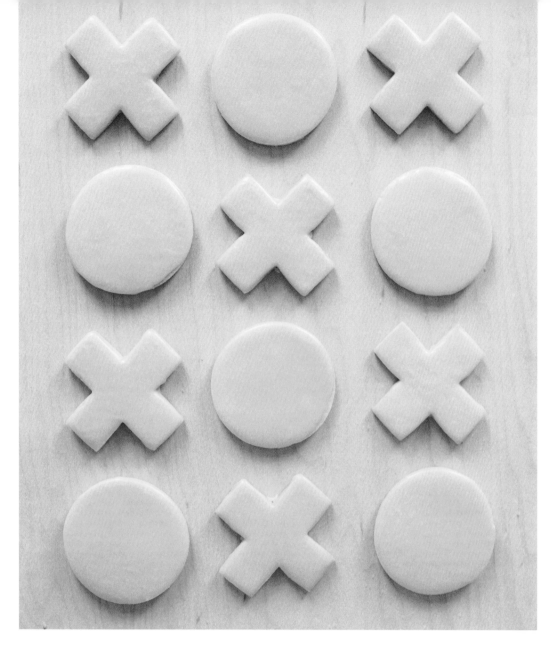

XOXO SUGAR COOKIES

Show your friends and family how much you care with these sugar
cookies inspired by hugs and kisses. Use an X-shaped cookie cutter
or make a paper template, then cut out the cookies with a knife.

INGREDIENTS

1½ cups (3 sticks) unsalted butter, at room temperature

2 cups granulated sugar

4 large eggs

1 teaspoon pure vanilla extract

5 cups all-purpose flour

2 teaspoons baking powder

1 teaspoon salt

2 cups confectioners' sugar

2 to 3 tablespoons water

Food coloring

DIRECTIONS

1. In a large bowl, combine butter and granulated sugar, and cream together with a hand mixer until smooth.

2. Add the eggs and vanilla, and beat until combined.

3. Stir in flour, baking powder, and salt.

4. Cover and chill in the fridge overnight, or for at least 2 hours.

5. Preheat the oven to 400°F. Line four baking sheets with parchment paper.

6. Roll out the dough on a floured surface until ¼ to ½ inch thick. Cut into "X" and "O" shapes using cookie cutters and/or paper templates. Set the cookies about 1 inch apart on the lined baking sheets.

7. Bake for 6 to 8 minutes, until the edges start to turn golden. Let cool completely.

8. To make the icing, whisk together the confectioners' sugar and 2 tablespoons of the water in a bowl. Tint with a drop of food coloring. If the icing is too thick, add the remaining 1 tablespoon water and whisk until smooth.

9. Dip the tops of the cooled cookies into the icing, and set on a wire rack until hardened, at least 2 to 3 hours, or up to overnight.

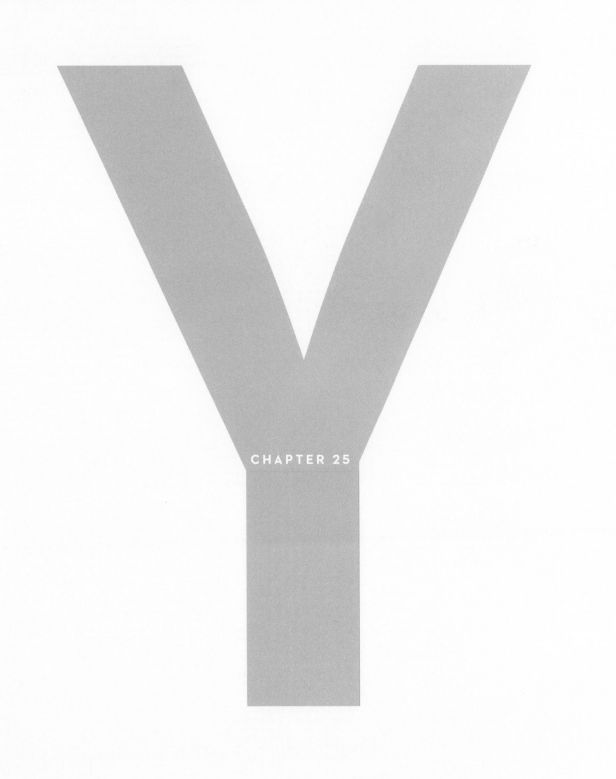

CHAPTER 25

YUMMY YOGURT PARFAITS

These healthy yogurt parfaits play on the flavors of the classic ice pop, contrasting sweet citrus and creamy vanilla yogurt. To make them easier to eat, you'll want to suprême larger citrus segments—that just means cutting the orange flesh from its membrane. Once you have the technique down, it comes in handy for everything from salads to desserts.

— MAKES 2 SERVINGS —

INGREDIENTS

2 cups citrus segments, from 3 navel oranges, 5 tangerines, or a mix of both (use a mix of tangerines and navel oranges for great flavor), plus more for garnish

2 tablespoons maple syrup

2 cups vanilla yogurt

DIRECTIONS

1. Grate the zest from one of the oranges, and peel 2 strips of zest from another one. Reserve.

2. Next, suprême any large citrus—no need to do this for mandarins or tangerines. Slice off the top and bottom of the fruit. Stand the fruit flat on your cutting board, and use downward strokes to cut off the peel and white pith, following the curve of the fruit and cutting off as much of the pith as possible without cutting into the flesh. Next, cut along the membrane to free the segments of fruit and discard the membrane.

3. Toss all the citrus in a bowl with grated zest and maple syrup. Let sit for 10 minutes.

4. To assemble the parfaits, spoon a layer of the yogurt into two 16-ounce glasses. Next, add a fruit layer with half the fruit, arranging the fruit so the widest edges sit against the glasses. Proceed with a yogurt layer, the remaining fruit, and then the remaining yogurt.

5. Garnish with a slice of orange and a twist of the reserved zest. Refrigerate for 30 minutes or up to 1 day, then serve.

CHAPTER 26

ZUCCHINI BREAD

This delicious bread is perfect for breakfast, brunch, or just an afternoon snack. Not overly sweet, it pairs perfectly with a hot cup of tea. The zucchini gives it a wonderfully moist texture.

— SERVES 9 —

INGREDIENTS

3 cups grated zucchini, pressed dry in a colander

1 2/3 cups sugar

2/3 cup vegetable oil

2 teaspoons pure vanilla extract

4 large eggs

3 cups flour

2 teaspoons baking soda

1 teaspoon table salt

1 teaspoon ground cinnamon

1/2 teaspoon ground cloves

1/2 teaspoon baking powder

1/2 cup chopped nuts

DIRECTIONS

1. Preheat the oven to 350°F. Grease a 9 by 5-inch loaf pan.

2. In a large bowl, mix the zucchini, sugar, vegetable oil, vanilla, and eggs until combined.

3. In another large bowl, combine the flour, baking soda, salt, cinnamon, cloves, and baking powder, and stir to combine.

4. Slowly pour the dry ingredients into the wet ingredients, and mix until just combined. Fold in the chopped nuts.

5. Pour the batter into the prepared loaf pan, and bake for 1 hour 10 minutes, or until a toothpick inserted into the center comes out clean.

6. Let cool in the pan for 2 hours before slicing.

ZUCCHINI CUPCAKES

Blueberries, lemony cream cheese frosting, and zucchini come together to create a deliciously moist cupcake. Sweet and tangy, these are cupcakes you're sure to enjoy.

— MAKES 12 TO 14 CUPCAKES —

INGREDIENTS

For the zucchini blueberry cupcakes

1½ cups grated zucchini

½ teaspoon sea salt, plus a pinch

1½ cups all-purpose flour

¼ teaspoon baking soda

¾ teaspoon baking powder

1 teaspoon ground cinnamon

½ teaspoon ground ginger

2 large eggs

1 cup granulated sugar

½ cup extra-virgin olive oil

1 cup blueberries

For the cream cheese frosting

4 ounces cream cheese, at room temperature

4 tablespoons (½ stick) unsalted butter, room temperature

1 teaspoon lemon zest

1 tablespoon fresh lemon juice

1½ cups confectioners' sugar, sifted

DIRECTIONS

1. To make the cupcakes, place the grated zucchini in a mesh strainer over a bowl. Toss with a pinch of sea salt. Tossing and pressing frequently, set the zucchini aside for 20 minutes or so to release its water.

2. Preheat the oven to 350°F. Line a 12-cup muffin tin with paper liners.

3. In a large bowl, combine the flour, baking soda, baking powder, cinnamon, ginger, and sea salt. In a small bowl, whisk together the eggs, granulated sugar, and olive oil. Fold in the drained zucchini. Stir the wet ingredients into the dry ingredients just until combined. Fold in the blueberries.

4. Spoon the batter into the prepared muffin tin, filling each well, about two-thirds full. Bake for 30 to 35 minutes, until the muffins are golden brown and the blueberries are bubbling and juicy. Let cool completely in the pan, 2 hours or longer.

5. To make the frosting, either in the bowl of a stand mixer fitted with the paddle attachment or in a large bowl using a handheld mixer, beat the cream cheese and butter on medium speed until pale and very fluffy, about 5 minutes. Add the lemon zest and lemon juice. With the mixer on low, gradually add the confectioners' sugar. Beat on low until the frosting is smooth and fluffy, about 3 minutes more.

6. Spoon the frosting into a zip-top bag. Cut a small hole from one corner. Working from the outside in, pipe the frosting in a spiral onto each cupcake. If the frosting becomes too soft, chill the cupcakes before serving.

7. Unfrosted cupcakes will keep in an airtight container at room temperature for 2 to 3 days. Frosted cupcakes should be eaten the same day.

ACKNOWLEDGMENTS

All the gratitude in my heart goes to the following superhumans who made the construction of this book possible.

First and foremost, the love of my life, cofounder of *Handmade Charlotte*, and cowriter of this book, Jonathan Faucett. His genius touches every single page. I also want to thank the brilliant *Handmade Charlotte* blog editor, manager, photographer, and award-winning crafter Kathleen Ballos. Her tremendous contribution made this book a reality!

I am sending big hugs to every *Handmade Charlotte* team member over the past decade, but especially to those who helped to create this book. This includes Virginia Stephenson, for her clever writing and infinite coolness. It also includes Eve Nettles, for instilling in me confidence to create the crafts that ended up in this super-big, happy book. Thank you also to Heather Donohue, our resident felting fairy, for delivering oatmeal cans of sunshine. And to Debbie Denomme, for crafting cheese and making lots of other juice box dreams. Colleen Farley, thank you for being awesome. And finally, to my editor, Sara Carder, and her right hand, Rachel Ayotte, for their patience and guidance.

I also want to send a billion thank-yous to my beautiful friends (and super BFFs) who are always there for me regardless of what space-traveling question I might throw their way.

Ashley Rush is a daily support beam, a moderator of our decades-long brainstorming session, and a constant source of inspiration. I also love you, Jane Mosbacher Morris! Jane has empowered me to write this book, answered every panicked call in every time zone she was saving the world in, and gave meaning to every purchase I made along my book-creating process. Thanks, Mama. Jeannine Harvey pointed me toward compassion for all mankind. Emily Meyer, style maven, mentor, and world opener, gave me confidence in my creative eye by allowing me to imitate hers. Gabrielle Blair is the mother of the internet and introduced me to everyone. I mean every single person in the world! Yes! I adore you. I am also so grateful to my expert craft squad, Amanda Kingloff and Jodi Levine, for their immense support.

Similarly, thank you so much, Debbie Henley and the Plaid family, for always believing in me. I am deeply grateful to Selina Meere for listening and providing honest feedback, and to Samantha Ettus for delivering inspired direction and validation when I needed it the most.

I also want to give double extra credit and five gold stars to my devoted family. This includes my twin sister, Rebecca Jensen-Diianni, and my brothers, Luke and Murphy Jensen. I am also so appreciative of my brother-in-law James Faucett's long weeks of editorial development. He was an essential gift at all the right times. Thank you also to my sister-in-law, Suzanne Poppe, for juggling, shuffling, and picking up the slack so that I could focus on the book. A magnitude of thanks also to my extended family, Margarita Cruz Hernandez and her family, for making my life better. There is a reason why I call her Saint Margarita. I love you so much. And to Charli (aka Charles) and Amy Shane. Thank you for loving us back and listening to a year of ideated educational theories filtered through a light spectrum.

Last, I want to acknowledge and give endless praise to my Ultimate Guide, Jesus. My faith and relationship with God gives me the courage to create and be my authentic self. It provides me with unbounded hope that my work and my contribution on this planet matter deeply.

PHOTO CREDITS

KATHLEEN BALLOS

Abacus Candy (page 5)

Acorn Matching Game (page 7)

Alligator Puppet (page 10)

Alphabet Magnets (page 15) (Original craft by Kersey Campbell)

Balloon Pop Game (page 21)

Beetles (page 26)

Binoculars (page 31)

Bird Feeder (page 33)

Bumblebee Slime Boxes (page 36)

Cactus (page 47)

Cookie-Cutter Candy Pops (page 53) (Original craft by Abby Hunter)

Charcoal (page 59)

Chewy Checkers (page 60)

Churro Action Figures (page 63)

Cucumber Cakes (page 66)

Daffodil Cupcakes (page 71)

Dioramas (page 72)

Diver Puppet (page 75)

Donut Bunnies (page 79)

Egg Party Favors (page 83)

Easy Embroidery (page 85)

Eraser Piñata (page 91)

Fingerprint Pumpkins (page 97)

Friendship Bracelets (page 106)

Flamingos (page 111)

Graduation Owls (page 118)

Hair Charms (page 131)

Hey Hey Cross-Stitch Magnets (page 141)

Horse in the Forest Cake (page 143)

Ice-Cream Charms (page 151)

Ice-Cream Puppet (page 154)

Jazzy Cassette People (page 165)

Jolly Storage Jars (page 167)

Key Chains (page 175)

Kitten Clutches (page 180)

Lovely Llamas (page 195)

Lobster Cupcakes (page 199)

Leaf Painting (page 191)

Mandala Cookie Tins (page 205)

Mouse Gift Box (page 215)

Night Sky Flashlight (page 224) (Original craft by Kersey Campbell)

Noodle Party (page 227)

Paper Bag Puppets (page 247)

Pasta Plants (page 251)

Patches (page 252)

Ping-Pong Bunny Cupcake Toppers (page 259)

Queen of Hearts Puppet (page 271) (Original craft by Caroline Gravino)

Rainbow Puppet (page 283)

Rock Puzzle (page 287)

Rocks on the Beach (page 289)

Salad Spinner Plates (page 295)

Sand Mill (page 297)

Sewing Cards (page 301)

Skee-Ball (page 307)

Stripy Storage (page 315)

Tie-Dye Tapestries (page 331)

Tops (page 335)

Tree Ornaments (page 337)

Under the Sea Macaroni Wreath (page 345)

Unicorn Puppet (page 351)

Urchin Ice Cream (page 355)

Valentine's Day Wreath (page 361)

Veggie Blocks (page 363) (Original craft
    by Gina Vide)

Walnut Llama Ornaments (page 373)

Watercolor Windsocks (page 377)

Watermelon Charms (page 381)

Wish Upon a Wreath Cake (page 385)

CAMILLA BRENCHLEY

Banana Puppets (page 23)

Envelopes (page 89)

Fortune Cookies (page 103)

Half Milks (page 133)

Invisible Ink (page 159)

Jam (page 170)

Kiss Art (page 178)

Lanterns (page 189)

Leaning Towers of Trapeze (step photos,
    page 193)

Lemon Bars (page 201)

Monkey Bread (page 219)

Neapolitan Treats (page 231) (Original
    recipe by Sandra Denneler)

Ornaments (page 239)

Olive Trading Beads (page 237)

Shibori Wall Hangings (page 305)

Swiss Cheese Fort (step photos, page 319)

Unexpected Encouragement (page 348)

Upside-Down Pineapple Cake (page 357)

Veggie Knots (page 365)

Victory Lap Village (page 369)

XOXO Sugar Cookies (page 393)

Zucchini Bread (page 401)

JONATHAN FAUCETT

Walrus Costume (page 374)

ABBY HUNTER

Award Ribbons (page 17)

Calla Lilies (page 50)

Gumdrop Swans (page 123)

Hot Potato (page 145)

Kokeshi Doll Stir Sticks (page 185)

Moon in Your Room (page 211)

Olive Stress Balls (page 235)

Peanut Party Favors (page 255)

Pretzel Necklace (page 265)

Rainbow Macaroni (page 281)

Tangram Piñata (page 327)

Turkey Party Favors (page 339)

MOLLIE JOHANSON

Flower Paper Clips (page 99)

Happy Mail Pencil Case (page 135)

Monograms (page 207)

Nature Bingo (page 223)

Quilt Magnets (page 275)

Solar System Necklace (page 311)

JODI LEVINE

Bunny Cupcakes (page 40)

Play Clay Sweet Shop (page 263)

ALLISON PEDIGO

Leaning Towers of Trapeze (page 193)
Swiss Cheese Fort (page 319)
Xylophone (page 389)

ELIZABETH STARK

Better Blondies (page 43)
Fancy French Toast (page 115)

Granola Bars (page 127)
Ice-Pop Monsters (page 157)
Ice Cream (page 161)
Milk Shakes (page 217)
Olive Oil Cherry Cake (page 243)
Raspberry-Mango Smoothies (page 291)
Slab Pie (page 321)
Yummy Yogurt Parfaits (page 397)
Zucchini Cupcakes (page 402)

PROJECT INDEX BY TYPE

CANDY CRAFTS, DECORATING
CAKES AND CUPCAKES

Abacus Candy (page 5)
Award Ribbons (page 17)
Bunny Cupcakes (page 40)
Calla Lilies (page 50)
Cookie-Cutter Candy Pops (page 53)
Daffodil Cupcakes (page 71)
Donut Bunnies (page 79)
Graduation Owls (page 118)
Gumdrop Swans (page 123)
Half Milks (page 133)
Horse in the Forest Cake (page 143)
Ice-Pop Monsters (page 157)
Kokeshi Doll Stir Sticks (page 185)
Lobster Cupcakes (page 199)
Ping-Pong Bunny Cupcake Toppers (page 259)
Rainbow Macaroni (page 281)
Wish Upon a Wreath Cake (page 385)

CHARMS, ACCESSORIES

Easy Embroidery (page 85)
Flower Paper Clips (page 99)
Friendship Bracelets (page 106)
Hair Charms (page 131)
Happy Mail Pencil Case (page 135)
Hey Hey Cross-Stitch Magnets (page 141)
Ice-Cream Charms (page 151)
Jazzy Cassette People (page 165)
Key Chains (page 175)
Kitten Clutches (page 180)
Monograms (page 207)
Patches (page 252)
Pretzel Necklace (page 265)
Solar System Necklace (page 311)
Urchin Ice Cream (page 355)
Watermelon Charms (page 381)

COSTUMES, PUPPETS

Alligator Puppet (page 10)
Banana Puppets (page 23)
Diver Puppet (page 75)
Ice-Cream Puppet (page 154)
Paper Bag Puppets (page 247)
Queen of Hearts Puppet (page 271)
Rainbow Puppet (page 283)
Unicorn Puppet (page 351)
Walrus Costume (page 374)

DÉCOR, ORNAMENTS,
WALL HANGINGS

Beetles (page 26)
Cactus (page 47)
Dioramas (page 72)
Fingerprint Pumpkins (page 97)

Flamingos (page 111)

Jolly Storage Jars (page 167)

Lovely Llamas (page 195)

Lanterns (page 189)

Mandala Cookie Tins (page 205)

Moon in Your Room (page 211)

Ornaments (page 239)

Pasta Plants (page 251)

Stripy Storage (page 315)

Shibori Wall Hangings (page 305)

Tree Ornaments (page 337)

Tie-Dye Tapestries (page 331)

Under the Sea Macaroni Wreath (page 345)

Valentine's Day Wreath (page 361)

Watercolor Windsocks (page 377)

Walnut Llama Ornaments (page 373)

GAMES, ACTIVITIES

Alphabet Magnets (page 15)

Acorn Matching Game (page 7)

Balloon Pop Game (page 21)

Chewy Checkers (page 60)

Churro Action Figures (page 63)

Charcoal (page 59)

Hot Potato (page 145)

Invisible Ink (page 159)

Leaning Towers of Trapeze (page 193)

Night Sky Flashlight (page 224)

Olive Trading Beads (page 237)

Olive Stress Balls (page 235)

Play Clay Sweet Shop (page 263)

Quilt Magnets (page 275)

Swiss Cheese Fort (page 319)

Sewing Cards (page 301)

Salad Spinner Plates (page 295)

Sand Mill (page 297)

Skee-Ball (page 307)

Tops (page 335)

Veggie Blocks (page 363)

Veggie Knots (page 365)

Victory Lap Village (page 369)

Xylophone (page 389)

GIFTS, LETTERS, SENTIMENTS

Envelopes (page 89)

Kiss Art (page 178)

Mouse Gift Box (page 215)

Unexpected Encouragement (page 348)

NATURE CRAFTS

Bird Feeder (page 33)

Leaf Painting (page 191)

Nature Bingo (page 223)

Rock Puzzle (page 287)

Rocks on the Beach (page 289)

PARTY CRAFTS, FAVORS

Binoculars (page 31)

Bumblebee Slime Boxes (page 36)

Eraser Piñata (page 91)

Egg Party Favors (page 83)

Fortune Cookies (page 103)

Noodle Party (page 227)

Peanut Party Favors (page 255)

Turkey Party Favors (page 339)

Tangram Piñata (page 327)

RECIPE INDEX BY TYPE

BREADS

Fancy French Toast (page 115)
Monkey Bread (page 219)
Zucchini Bread (page 401)

CAKES, CUPCAKES

Neapolitan Treats (page 231)
Olive Oil Cherry Cake (page 243)
Upside-Down Pineapple Cake (page 357)
Zucchini Cupcakes (page 402)

COOKIES

Better Blondies (page 43)
XOXO Sugar Cookies (page 393)

DRINKS

Milk Shake (page 217)
Raspberry-Mango Smoothies (page 291)

FRUIT DESSERTS

Jam (page 170)
Lemon Bars (page 201)
Slab Pie (page 321)

ICE CREAM

Ice Cream (page 161)

SNACKS

Cucumber Cakes (page 66)
Granola Bars (page 127)
Yummy Yogurt Parfaits (page 397)

SEASONAL AND HOLIDAY INDEX

SUMMER

Alligator Puppet (page 10)

Award Ribbons (page 17)

Banana Puppets (page 23)

Beetles (page 26)

Binoculars (page 31)

Bumblebee Slime Boxes (page 36)

Cactus (page 47)

Cookie-Cutter Candy Pops (page 53)

Charcoal (page 59)

Dioramas (page 72)

Diver Puppet (page 75)

Easy Embroidery (page 85)

Friendship Bracelets (page 106)

Horse in the Forest Cake (page 143)

Hot Potato (page 145)

Ice-Cream Charms (page 151)

Ice-Cream Puppet (page 154)

Ice-Pop Monsters (page 157)

Invisible Ink (page 159)

Ice Cream (page 161)

Lanterns (page 189)

Lovely Llamas (page 195)

Lobster Cupcakes (page 199)

Moon in Your Room (page 211)

Night Sky Flashlight (page 224)

Noodle Party (page 227)

Neapolitan Treats (page 231)

Olive Stress Balls (page 235)

Olive Trading Beads (page 237)

Patches (page 252)

Peanut Party Favors (page 255)

Play Clay Sweet Shop (page 263)

Rainbow Puppet (page 283)

Rocks on the Beach (page 289)

Salad Spinner Plates (page 295)

Sand Mill (page 297)

Stripy Storage (page 315)

Raspberry-Mango Smoothies (page 291)

Tie-Dye Tapestries (page 331)

Tops (page 335)

Under the Sea Macaroni Wreath (page 345)

Unicorn Puppet (page 351)

Upside-Down Pineapple Cake (page 357)

Veggie Blocks (page 363)

Watercolor Windsocks (page 377)

Watermelon Charms (page 381)

Xylophone (page 389)

Yummy Yogurt Parfaits (page 397)

SUMMER HOLIDAYS—FATHER'S DAY

Jazzy Cassette People (page 165)

SUMMER HOLIDAYS—FOURTH OF JULY

Balloon Pop Game (page 21)

Skee-Ball (page 307)

FALL

Acorn Matching Game (page 7)

Better Blondies (page 43)

Hey Hey Cross-Stitch Magnets (page 141)

Jolly Storage Jars (page 167)

Jam (page 170)

Leaf Painting (page 191)

Milk Shake (page 217)

Monkey Bread (page 219)

Paper Bag Puppets (page 247)

Quilt Magnets (page 275)

Zucchini Bread (page 401)

Zucchini Cupcakes (page 402)

FALL—BACK-TO-SCHOOL

Abacus Candy (page 5)

Alphabet Magnets (page 15)

Envelopes (page 89)

Eraser Piñata (page 91)

Granola Bars (page 127)

Happy Mail Pencil Case (page 135)

Key Chains (page 175)

Monograms (page 207)

Solar System Necklace (page 311)

Unexpected Encouragement (page 348)

FALL HOLIDAYS—HALLOWEEN

Fingerprint Pumpkins (page 97)

Flamingos (page 111)

Walrus Costume (page 374)

FALL HOLIDAYS—THANKSGIVING

Slab Pie (page 321)

Turkey Party Favors (page 339)

WINTER

Chewy Checkers (page 60)

Fortune Cookies (page 103)

Fancy French Toast (page 115)

Gumdrop Swans (page 123)

Half Milks (page 133)

Leaning Tower of Trapeze (page 193)

Olive Oil Cherry Cake (page 243)

Swiss Cheese Fort (page 319)

Shibori Wall Hangings (page 305)

Victory Lap Village (page 369)

WINTER HOLIDAYS—CHRISTMAS

Mandala Cookie Tins (page 205)

Mouse Gift Box (page 215)

Ornaments (page 239)

Walnut Llama Ornaments (page 373)

Tree Ornaments (page 337)

Urchin Ice Cream (page 355)

WINTER HOLIDAYS—VALENTINE'S DAY

Kiss Art (page 178)

Queen of Hearts Puppet (page 271)

Valentine's Day Wreath (page 361)

XOXO Sugar Cookies (page 393)

SPRING

Bird Feeder (page 33)

Cucumber Cakes (page 66)

Flower Paper Clips (page 99)

Graduation Owls (page 118)

Kitten Clutches (page 180)

Kokeshi Doll Stir Sticks (page 185)

Lemon Bars (page 201)

Nature Bingo (page 223)

Pretzel Necklace (page 265)
Rock Puzzle (page 287)
Sewing Cards (page 301)
Tangram Piñata (page 327)
Veggie Knots (page 365)

SPRING HOLIDAYS—ST. PATRICK'S DAY

Hair Charms (page 131)
Rainbow Macaroni (page 281)

SPRING HOLIDAYS—EASTER

Bunny Cupcakes (page 40)
Calla Lilies (page 50)

Daffodil Cupcakes (page 71)
Donut Bunnies (page 79)
Egg Party Favors (page 83)
Ping-Pong Bunny Cupcake Toppers (page 259)

SPRING HOLIDAYS—CINCO DE MAYO

Churro Action Figures (page 63)

SPRING HOLIDAYS—MOTHER'S DAY

Pasta Plants (page 251)
Wish Upon a Wreath Cake (page 385)

ABOUT THE AUTHOR

Rachel Faucett is the mother of five extremely creative children and loves everyone she meets. When she's not in her garden or craft studio, she's moving furniture about the house. Faucett was named in Business Insider's "Top 20 Most Influential Pinterest Users," *Country Living*'s "Top 100 Most Creative People," and Disney Interactive's "Best Kids' Craft Site." The author's fun projects have been featured in numerous online and print magazines worldwide. She also designs for brands like Anthropologie, Pottery Barn Kids, To the Market, and Plaid Crafts.